23.70

3/04

DOLLEY MADISON
America's First Lady

DOLLEY MADISON
America's First Lady

Myra Weatherly

620 South Elm Street, Suite 223
Greensboro, North Carolina   27406
http://www.morganreynolds.com

DOLLEY MADISON: AMERICA'S FIRST LADY

Library of Congress Cataloging-in-Publication Data

Weatherly, Myra.
  Dolley Madison : America's First Lady / Myra Weatherly.-- 1st ed.
    p. cm.
Summary: A biography of Dolley Madison, the wife of the fourth president
of the United States.
Includes bibliographical references and index.
  ISBN 1-883846-95-1 (library binding)
  1. Madison, Dolley, 1768-1849--Juvenile literature. 2. Presidents'
spouses--United States--Biography--Juvenile literature. [1. Madison,
Dolley, 1768-1849. 2. First ladies. 3. Women--Biography.] I. Title.
  E342.1 .W43 2003
  973.5'1'092--dc21

                              2002008147

Printed in the United States of America
First Edition

Notable Americans

Dolley Madison

Thomas Jefferson

John Adams

Andrew Jackson

Alexander Hamilton

George W. Bush

Lyndon Baines Johnson

Dwight D. Eisenhower

Ishi

Richard Nixon

Madeleine Albright

Lou Henry Hoover

Thurgood Marshall

Petticoat Spies

William Tecumseh Sherman

Mary Todd Lincoln

For
Christa Carter

Contents

Dolley Madison, 1812
(Courtesy of the Library of Congress.)

Chapter One

Quaker Maid

In the spring of 1775, rumblings of revolution stirred in the American colonies of Great Britain. To seven-year-old Dolley Payne, who loved to stroll through the Virginia countryside, talk of war meant little. She was more interested in the colorful wildflowers peeking through the underbrush and the blossoming dogwoods that lined the path to the Cedar Creek Quaker School.

Dolley loved colorful objects. Like all Quaker girls, Dolley wore a plain, gray dress that reached to her toes and a drab, billowy bonnet tied under her chin. The Quaker religion—also known as the Society of Friends—did not permit members to wear colorful fabrics, lace, ruffles, ribbons, or jewelry. Her mother insisted that she wear a white linen mask to protect her fair face from "ugly freckles" and mitts to keep her hands white.

Dolley was a good Quaker—but she had one secret. Beneath her plain dress hung a precious treasure—a glittering piece of jewelry. Grandmother Payne, who was not a Quaker, had given it to Dolley. To keep it safe and out of sight, Dolley placed the jewelry in a little bag that she sewed to a piece of string and concealed beneath her frock.

One day, as she was sitting on a hard school bench, she felt for the forbidden piece of jewelry, but it was not there. On the way home, a frantic search among the pine needles that carpeted the path ended in desperation. It was lost.

Dolley would never lose her love for beautiful things. The experience of losing her first piece of jewelry made such an impression on her that she never forgot it. She talked about the bauble—as she called it—until the end of her life.

Although Dolley grew up in Virginia, she was born in a two-room log house in the wilderness of Guilford County, North Carolina. Her parents, John and Mary Coles Payne, came from elite Virginia families. Three years prior to Dolley's birth, John and Mary Payne left colonial Virginia to join the New Garden Quaker pioneer settlement in North Carolina. Mary Payne grew up in a Quaker family, but John Payne was a convert. When the Paynes first moved into their North Carolina log house, they had one son, Walter. A second son, William Temple, was born a year later. Then on May 20, 1768, came their first daughter, Dolley. Before Dolley was a year old, the Paynes ended their four-year stay in the North Carolina colony. John Payne sold his land holdings of over 283 acres, and the family took the wagon trail back to New Hanover County, Virginia.

Back in Virginia, John Payne reclaimed a small farm

New Garden Meeting House and Revolutionary Oak, 1791, as painted by John Collins in 1869. *(Courtesy of the Friends Historical Collection, Guilford College, Greensboro, N.C.)*

at Little Bird Creek. He and his wife were soon appointed clerks of the Cedar Creek Quaker Meeting. Their duties included keeping accurate minutes, records, and documents pertaining to births, marriages, and deaths. Members of the Society of Friends believe that God speaks to a person's soul, called the Inner Light. Quakers believe in social justice and refuse to bear arms against their fellow men. Members of the Society of Friends suffered dire persecutions in England. As a result, many of them fled to the American colonies.

In 1775, seven-year-old Dolley and her family moved to nearby Scotchtown, a large tobacco plantation with a big, rambling house. The clapboard house, with a dungeon beneath, had once been the manor house of a large Scottish settlement. Back of the splendid nine-teen-room house stood the stables and slave cabins. The open fields served as an ideal place for Dolley and her brothers to run races.

John Payne's plantation, like most others of his day, was self-sustaining. Nearly everything needed for life grew on the farm. The Paynes purchased only a few staples, such as tea or sugar. Plantation owners raised sheep for wool. They spun flax into linen for clothing. Farmers grew some cotton, but ginning cotton by hand was a slow process. Each plantation had its own blacksmith's shop, carpenter's shop, and flour mill. Large plantations depended on slave labor. John Payne's estate was no exception—he owned about fifty slaves. In addition to working in the fields, slaves tended the gardens and helped run the household by caring for the children, cooking, and cleaning.

In later years, Dolley recalled life at Scotchtown. She shared a green and white bedroom with her sister Lucy. Her most vivid memory was of the living room where the family gathered in the evenings. Fireplaces with black marble mantels from Scotland dominated two corners of the large room.

Even as a child, Dolley enjoyed people. Her memories of visitors to Scotchtown were happy ones. Legend has it that when her cousin Patrick Henry (who later became famous for saying, "Give me liberty or give me death") came to visit, he roasted chestnuts in the fire and always had a candy pull with the children.

Although Scotchtown became highly successful, the

Dolley's cousin Patrick Henry was a leader in the American Revolution.
(Courtesy of the Library of Congress.)

issue of slavery weighed heavily on John and Mary Payne. Quakers held to the doctrine that slavery was wrong. In 1769, the year the Paynes returned to Virginia, the members of the Cedar Creek Meeting "unanimously agreed that something be done about it." However, Virginia laws made it illegal to free slaves.

After the signing of the Declaration of Independence in 1776, the Quakers wrote to Governor Patrick Henry, seeking help in ending slavery. He issued the following statement: "We ought to lament and deplore the necessity of holding our fellow-men in bondage. Believe me, I shall honor the Quakers for their notable efforts to abolish slavery." Yet, it would be almost another hundred years before the practice ended.

In 1782, the Virginia legislature passed a law making it legal to free slaves, and Dolley's parents were among the first Quakers to do so. Already unpopular because of their antiwar stands, the Quakers became more despised by their slaveholding neighbors. As the tensions intensified, many Quakers moved north to free states.

The Payne family decided to leave their comfortable plantation for Philadelphia, Pennsylvania. John Payne sold the estate. As Dolley watched the distribution of legal documents that freed the slaves, one member of the household refused to leave. The children's nurse, Mother Amy, insisted on accompanying them as a paid servant. Mother Amy never spent her salary and later willed the money to Mary Payne. In May 1783, two years after the American Revolution had ended, the Payne family left the Virginia countryside for the largest city in America.

Chapter Two

Life in Philadelphia

Although Scotchtown had been isolated from the violence of the Revolutionary War, Dolley saw weary faces and crippled veterans on the streets of Philadelphia. The long conflict had left much destruction, but the colonies were free. Now what should be done? Would the states unify into a single nation or continue to be a loose arrangment of thirteen soverign states? These were the question being asked everywhere, especially in Philadelphia, the city that had served as the capital during the revolution.

Dolley found life quite different in Philadelphia, the most exciting city in the American colonies. In 1783, the bustling city of more than thirty thousand people had a college, a medical school, a hospital, a library, a theater, a home for the aged, a volunteer fire department, a prison, and several schools for young girls. Dolley said, "In my first thirty minutes in Philadelphia, I saw more people than I had observed in all of my previous life." The cultural atmosphere was due in large part to the influence and genius of Benjamin Franklin, who spent most of his life in Philadelphia. Compared to the quiet of Scotchtown, it seemed crowded and noisy.

Until they found a home, the Paynes stayed with a prosperous Quaker family, the Henry Drinkers. After a short stay with the Drinkers, they moved into a tall, narrow brick building in a connected row of houses. Their home, identical to the others on the block, had two stories, an attic, and a tiny porch in front—and not one sprig of grass.

The Payne home was small and cramped. The first floor had two rooms. The front section served as office space for John Payne's starch business. The family used the back room for dining and entertaining guests. Dolley and her three sisters shared one of the two upstairs bedrooms, while the three boys and Mother Amy slept in the attic. Philadelphia row houses in the eighteenth century had kitchen additions in the rear.

In spite of the inconveniences, country-bred Dolley found the sights and sounds of city life captivating. Wide eyed, she watched the endless stream of carriage and stagecoach traffic wind through the narrow cobblestone streets. Cries of street vendors added to the clatter of horses' hooves. Chimes of church bells filled the air—a reminder that Philadelphia was a place of religious tolerance. When the night noises ceased at ten o'clock, the town watchmen took up their hourly cry, "All is well."

Dolley and her new friend Sally Drinker roamed the city streets, gazing at the elegant, colorful hats and

Dolley Payne enjoyed the hubbub of Philadelphia life.
(Courtesy of the Library of Congress)

dresses displayed in store windows. In her plain, gray dress and bonnet, Dolley often observed the well-dressed Philadelphia society ladies strolling along Chestnut Street in the afternoons. Dolley's Quaker upbringing did not keep her from wishing for beautiful clothes. Even the men wore brightly colored waistcoats, silk stockings, and silver buckles on their shoes.

Sally Drinker pointed out the city landmarks to Dolley. The famous chimes in Christ Church came from England. The Continental Congress first met and adopted the Articles of Confederation in Carpenter's Hall. The Declaration of Independence had been signed in the State House—later known as Independence Hall and the home of the Liberty Bell. On the banks of the Delaware was the "Treaty Elm" where William Penn made a treaty with a group of Native Americans for the land he called Pennsylvania.

City life brought many changes to Dolley's world. Philadelphia Quakers were not as strict as those in Virginia. Dolley had many Quaker friends. One who knew her at this time recalled fifty years later that "she came upon our cold hearts in Philadelphia, suddenly and unexpectedly, with all the delightful influences of a summer sun from the sweet South in the month of May." She socialized on the front stoop with her Quaker neighbors in the summer evenings and enjoyed innocent amusements such as parties, picnics, fishing, and ice-skating on the Schuylkill River in winter.

Dolley loved visiting the Creighton family in Haddonfield, New Jersey. Haddonfield was an old

Philadelphia, the largest city in the United States, offered Dolley many different experiences from those she had had in rural Virginia. *(Courtesy of the Library of Congress.)*

Quaker community, more cultured than most. She made the fifteen-mile trip by coach and horse-ferry. The Creightons ran a public inn on the King's Highway for travelers on their way to New York. Everyday there were new visitors. Getting to know many non-Quakers broadened Dolley's outlook on life.

Often the Creighton children and Dolley would hop onto the rear of a jouncing mail coach and ride for a mile or so. They would then leap off and walk back to the village. Of course, Dolley never told her mother of these excursions. Long afterward, one of the boys in

Haddonfield remembered popular Dolley as "being of slight figure, possessing a delicate oval face and nose tilted like a flower, jet black hair, and blue eyes of wondrous sweetness."

Dolley's appearance sometimes caused jealousy among girls her own age. At the age of sixteen, she was tall and exceptionally pretty by the standards of her day. Her plump figure attracted the attention of men whenever she walked down the street, and she received countless compliments. Once, Benjamin Franklin, known as an admirer of attractive girls, peered through his bifocals at Dolley and pronounced, "You are the most beautiful young lady in America, and I have never met your equal in Paris or London." Dolley could still quote the compliment verbatim a half century later.

Clearly, Dolley Payne did not lack eligible suitors. But in the eighteenth century when girls usually married in their teens, Dolley said she "never meant to marry." Likely, she was displaying her independent spirit, or she may have deferred thoughts of marriage because she was needed at home.

The new life in Philadelphia was far more difficult for her parents than for Dolley. Freeing the slaves had been a costly undertaking for John Payne. Living expenses proved to be far greater in Philadelphia than on a plantation. Unfortunately, the formerly successful Virginia farmer lacked experience for running a city business. He had set up a laundry starch plant on the ground floor of the row house soon after arriving in Philadelphia, but the business venture faced trouble from the start. Times were hard and people bought only the ne-

Benjamin Franklin once complimented Dolley Payne on her good looks.
(Courtesy of the Library of Congress.)

cessities of life. For many people, starch was a luxury item they could forego. John Payne also invested heavily in a land company and lost money. To make the situation even worse, an infant daughter, named Philadelphia, after their new home, died.

John and Mary Payne quickly became leaders in the Pine Street Monthly Meeting of Philadelphia. As elder and lay preacher, John Payne enjoyed more prestige in the religious community in Philadelphia than he had at Cedar Creek Meeting in Virginia.

As eldest daughter, Dolley did all she could to ease the family's burdens by helping with the younger children, the housekeeping, and the cooking. She became a skilled seamstress and haunted the fabric shops, buying remnants and scraps of expensive material. She deftly blended pieces of dark silk and velvet into somber costumes so as to be acceptable in the Quaker community.

In 1787, most of the city's attention was on the convention being held that summer. Beginning on May 25, five days after Dolley's nineteenth birthday, delegates from most of the thirteen separate states gathered for a federal convention in the State House. Under the weak central government agreed to in the Articles of Confederation, many issues, such as trade and the repayment of the money borrowed during the war, created tension between the states. It was almost impossible to form a cohesive foreign policy with thirteen autonomous governments, and even friendly European nations hesitated to loan more money to the new government for fear that it would not be paid back. As the problems mounted, there slowly developed a consensus that the Articles of Confederation needed to be revised. The states agreed to send delegates back to Philadelphia to discuss ways to fix the problems. After a hot summer of arguments and compromise, the federal convention agreed to create a new constitution.

As the delegates trickled into the city, some held to the conviction that each state should be sovereign and that the national government should be weak; others insisted that a much stronger central government should be established.

During the summer of 1787, Dolley and other Philadelphians sometimes caught glimpses of George Washington, Benjamin Franklin, Alexander Hamilton, and other notables strolling the city streets—but they had no idea what went on behind the closed doors of Independence Hall. The delegates voted for secrecy, to avoid outside influences, and even kept the windows closed during the hottest days of summer. Years later, Dolley would learn that one delegate named James Madison kept a daily record of every speech and action made inside the hall.

After much debate, wrangling, and compromise, the delegates wrote a new constitution that was adopted in September. The Constitution called for a stronger central government and held out the promise of solving many of the problems that had plagued the states. But the battle for a new government was far from over. Before the Constitution could become law, it had to be ratified by at least nine states. Bitter arguments for and against ratification took place throughout the thirteen states. James Madison joined with John Jay and Alexander Hamilton from New York and published a series of articles explaining why the new Constitution fitted the principles that had been fought for in the American Revolution. These promotional essays were published in newspapers and later came to be known as the *Federalist Papers.*

James Madison was the principal designer of the Constitution and its most eloquent supporter. When he promised that the Bill of Rights would be added during the first session of the new Congress, a majority of the states ratified the document that many called "Mr. Madison's Constitution." Now there would be a federal government with executive, legislative, and judicial branches. George Washington was elected the first president, and the fast-growing city of New York became the first capital. The capital would soon move to Philadelphia and later would be located south in what was then Virginia, on the banks of the Potomoc River.

While the new government was being established, John Payne's starch business continued to lose money. In 1789, he declared bankruptcy—a humilitation for the Payne family. His fellow Quakers "read him out of meeting," forcing him to give up his church membership, because he could not pay his debts. John Payne retreated to his second-floor bedroom and seldom emerged. Dolley, however, had no intention of brooding over her family's financial situation. She was determined to do something about it.

Chapter Three

Marriage to John Todd

In 1789, Dolley Payne turned twenty-one—an age by which most young women in her time were already married. While she had many admirers and several proposals, she had refused all of them. The most persistent of her suitors was John Todd, a Quaker and successful lawyer. He spent several years courting Dolley. Then, during her father's bankruptcy and expulsion from the Pine Street Meeting, John Todd stood by John Payne's side. This endeared Todd to Dolley, and she accepted his marriage proposal.

On January 7, 1790, twenty-two-year-old Dolley married twenty-seven-year-old John Todd. The traditional Quaker wedding, a simple affair with no music or flowers, took place at Pine Street Meeting House with Eliza Collins and Anthony Morris as attendants. The couple pledged their devotion and loyalty to each other. Afterwards, they signed an official marriage certificate. Eighty wedding guests added their signatures.

As John and Dolley set up housekeeping on Chestnut Street, Philadelphia buzzed with activity. The capital of the United States had moved from New York back to Philadelphia. Ten years would pass before the government moved to the new Washington City. Meanwhile, President George Washington was house hunting in the City of Brotherly Love. Congressmen looked for rooms to rent and merchants boosted prices.

Taking advantage of the increase in rents caused by the surge in population, Dolley's mother opened her home to boarders. Mary Payne did not limit her boarders to Quakers. During their frequent visits to the Payne boardinghouse, Dolley and John came to know one boarder from New York, Senator Aaron Burr.

With the return of Congress to Philadelphia, John Todd's legal practice prospered. In 1791, he purchased a three-story brick house at Fourth and Walnut that served as a combination office and residence. The Todds furnished the house with luxuries—in sharp contrast to the Quaker creed of simplicity. Dolley bought carpets, mahogany tables, Windsor chairs, mirrors, and a cabinet to display china and crystal—fine things she had always longed to have. Todd provided a horse and riding chair for Dolley to use when visiting friends.

At the time of the move to Fourth Street, Dolley was expecting her first child. On February 29, 1792, she gave birth to a son they named John Payne after Dolley's father. The boy was called Payne. "There is no other infant like him in all the world," Dolley confided to her longtime friend, Eliza Collins.

After their meeting in Philadelphia, Eliza Collins and Dolley Madison became lifelong friends. *(From* The Life and Letters of Dolley Madison *by Allen C. Clark, 1914.)*

Shortly after Payne's birth, Dolley's father died. Since his business had failed, he had spent the past three years depressed and living alone in his room. For a man who had lived most of his life as a strict Quaker, he had few mourners at his funeral. His family and a few friends gave parting tributes. Dolley not only grieved for her father, but for Mother Amy as well, who died a short time later. Dolley felt she had lost two parents.

Family and friends comforted Dolley. She adored motherhood and had a devoted husband. Her sister Anna came to live with the Todds following John Payne's death. Her social life in the active, new capital of the United States widened her circle of friends. She even began to wear clothes that were not the traditional Quaker gray. Dolley attended Martha Washington's socials and found the president's wife to be charming.

In the summer of 1793, Dolley's fifteen-year-old sister Lucy eloped with seventeen-year-old George Steptoe Washington, the president's nephew. Young George Steptoe had been brought to Philadelphia by his uncle to attend college. While living at Mary Payne's boardinghouse, he and Lucy fell in love. George Steptoe, heir to Harewood, a fine Virginia estate, was not a Quaker—a disappointment to Mrs. Payne. Because of her marriage, Lucy was read out of the Pine Street Meeting.

That same summer, Dolley gave birth to another son, William Temple. Within days of the baby's birth, an epidemic of yellow fever struck Philadelphia. No one was safe. Some victims died within hours, none lasted more than a few days. In 1793, doctors did not know the cause of the disease, or how to treat it. Some tried bleeding the patients; other doctors used a West Indian remedy made from bark and wine. Nothing worked. Hundreds of people—rich and poor, young and old, free and slave—died each day.

Distinguished physician Benjamin Rush noted in his diary that mosquitoes were "uncommonly numerous" in Philadelphia at the time of the epidemic. However, another century passed before researchers discovered that mosquitoes carried the disease. Not knowing that mosquitoes carried the virus, people avoided contact with one another. They refused to shake hands and walked in the middle of the street covering their mouths and noses with vinegar-soaked rags.

Panic erupted as people fled the city. Dr. Rush wrote in his diary: "Parents desert their children as soon as they are infected . . . Many people thrust their parents into the streets as soon as they complain of a headache . . . Friendship is nearly banished from our city." Government officials joined the mass exodus. Secretary of State Thomas Jefferson stayed behind because he felt some member of the administration should be in place. At the beginning of the epidemic, Jefferson wrote to a friend, "Everyone is leaving the city who can."

Among the exodus that clogged the roads out of the city was a litter bearing Dolley, still weak from childbirth, and her newborn son. After settling Dolley, the children, and Mary Payne at Gray's Ferry, a popular resort area on the Schuylkill River, John Todd returned to the plague-stricken city. He prepared wills for his clients and nursed his parents through the stages of the disease—raging fever, chills, delirium, yellowed flesh, bleeding, and finally the black vomit that signaled death. John's father died on October 3 and his mother on October 12. John Todd continued to minister to the needs of Philadelphians until October 24, when he saddled his horse and headed for Gray's Ferry to see his beloved Dolley and the boys.

On the way to the country, John became ill with yellow fever—he knew the symptoms too well. At last, he reached the house where Dolley was staying. Mary Payne opened the door. "I feel the fever in my veins, but I must see *her* once more," he gasped. Dolley ran down the steps and caught her husband in her arms as he sagged to the floor. A few hours later, John Todd died.

On the same day, Baby William died of an unknown cause. Dolley became desperately ill and remained sick for days. She was probably suffering from shock and grief over losing her husband and baby; the length of her illness indicates that she had not contracted yellow fever. Mrs. Payne nursed her daughter through confusion, nightmares, and near-unconsciousness. Eventually, Dolley recovered enough to turn her attention to little Payne, who now became the center of her world.

Recuperating at Gray's Ferry, Dolley had to deal with new financial worries. Her mother wrote to the Todd family nurse in Philadelphia that Dolley was "nearly moneyless having only nineteen Dollars Left and a number of other Debts to pay before she can move

. . . and if her poor Dear husband left any money with thee contrive to send it to her . . . "

Shortly before his death in July, John Todd had made a will appointing "my dear Wife Executrix of this my will." Dolley, however, had not received a penny of her inheritance. John's brother James had not only taken possession of his parents' estate but also of John's papers. In response to Dolley's repeated requests for her husband's papers, including the will, James Todd suggested that she sell John's books. She replied: "I was hurt my dear Jamy that the Idea of his Library should occur as a proper source for raising money— Books from which he wished his child improved, shall remain sacred, and I would feel the pinching hand of poverty before I disposed of them."

Dolley assumed full responsibility for providing for her family. As the weeks dragged on, it became clear that James Todd intended to deprive her of her rightful share of her husband's and mother-in-law's estates. She hired a lawyer to assist her and demanded the papers be sent to her. It would take a year before full settlement was made.

Chapter Four

Return to the City

By December 1793, the yellow fever epidemic had abated. The young widow Dolley Todd, along with little Payne and her thirteen-year-old sister Anna, moved back into her home on Chestnut Street. Because of Dolley's persistence, she received a partial settlement of part of her inheritance. It was enough money and property to be free of fears of poverty.

The epidemic killed five thousand citizens out of a city of thirty thousand, and another seventeen thousand had fled. When Washington returned for his second term in office, there were no welcoming crowds in the streets. Slowly people returned and Philadelphia became less of a ghost town. Government officials reappeared, the market reopened, shops conducted business as usual, and newspapers reported on the heated arguments in Congress that continued as if they had never been interrupted.

The widow Todd faced new responsibilities as head

of a family. No one from her family remained to advise her. Dolley's mother had yielded to Lucy and George Steptoe Washington's request that she, eleven-year-old Mary, and ten-year-old John live with them at Harewood in Virginia. In the absence of family, Dolley spent time with old friends.

First Lady Martha Washington called on Dolley to offer condolences on the loss of her husband and infant son. Vice President John Adams and his wife also visited. Abigail Adams later wrote that she was "much impressed with the great & gallant spirit" shown by Dolley. Other high-ranking government visitors included Secretary of State Thomas Jefferson and Attorney General Edmund Randolph. Secretary of War Henry Knox and Chief Justice of the Supreme Court John Jay also offered their condolences.

As spring emerged, Dolley began to put the mourning behind her and return to her vivacious self. Suitors began to call again. She was twenty-five years old and attractive. "Gentlemen would station themselves where they could see her pass," said her closest friend Eliza Collins, who accompanied Dolley on walks about town. Once Eliza teased Dolley, "Really, Dolley, thou must hide thy face, there are so many staring at thee."

It was on one of these walks in May of 1794 that James Madison noticed Dolley for the first time. He was taken by the beautiful lady, who was seventeen years his junior. Madison, who up to this point had been a confirmed bachelor, asked his fellow congressman Aaron Burr to introduce him to Dolley. Dolley had recently signed a will making Burr guardian of her son.

Dolley wrote to Eliza Collins: "Thou must come to me. Aaron Burr says that the great little Madison has asked to be brought to see me this evening." Eliza, detecting a hint of romance, readily agreed to act as chaperone. When a man in the eighteenth century arranged a visit with a lady through a third party, he was making his romantic intentions clear.

With Eliza by her side, Dolley received the two guests in her home. Dolley chose not to wear Quaker gray for the occasion. Eliza reported that her friend was dressed "in a mulberry-colored satin, with a silk tulle kerchief over her neck, and on her head an exquisitely dainty little cap, from which an occasional uncropped curl would escape." The candlelight and gleaming silver set off her appearance.

The two men who bowed before her were both slight, but the resemblance ended there. The flamboyant and charming Burr liked flashy clothes; Dolley noted that Madison, soft-voiced and five feet four inches tall, wore a "black suit of seemly cut, a white shirt and black stockings of silk, with buckles of silver upon his shoes."

Reportedly, the topics of conversation during this eventful meeting included the Philadelphia weather, the poor quality of French silk, and the mounting grievances against Great Britain's treatment of the former colonies. Burr talked in a glib, self-assured, and argumentative manner while Madison's speech was courteous, deliberate, and full of facts and figures—and always delivered with a twinkle in his slate blue eyes.

Aaron Burr introduced James Madison to Dolley Payne Todd.
(Courtesy of the Library of Congress.)

Before leaving, Madison invited Dolley and Payne to go riding with him in the country.

Dolley felt honored to receive attention from James Madison. At age forty-three, he had won a national reputation for his work at the Constitutional Convention, was the leader of the Congress, and was also highly regarded in Europe as one of the greatest political minds of the era.

Now the brilliant Madison was in love with the widow Dolley Payne Todd. Determined to win her affections, Madison began to visit two or three times a week, and then daily. He usually brought a gift for Dolley or a toy for Payne. Within a month of their first meeting, James asked Dolley to marry him. She did not say no, nor did she say yes. Her husband had been dead less than a year, and she knew that if she married Madison, a non-Quaker, she would be read out of the Society of Friends, the very people who had sustained her during her grief. But she had grown to feel strongly for Madison and knew he would be a good husband and father.

Their courtship became a topic of conversation in Philadelphia. Martha Washington invited Dolley to tea and asked, "Dolley, is it true that you are engaged to James Madison?" Taken aback, the young widow stammered that she thought not. Mrs. Washington continued: "If it is so . . . he will make thee a good husband, and all the better for being so much older . . . The esteem and friendship existing between Mr. Madison and my husband is very great, and we would wish thee to be happy."

When he met Dolley Todd, James Madison was already a well-known statesman.
(Courtesy of the Library of Congress.)

In June, Dolley informed Madison that she would visit relatives in Virginia and take the time to make a final decision. She would have her answer sometime during the summer. Accompanied by Anna and Payne, Dolley caught a stagecoach to Hanover County where she wrestled with the problem at her Aunt Lucy and Uncle Isaac Winston's plantation, near her childhood home of Scotchtown.

Meanwhile, James Madison went home to Montpelier. He had plenty of work to do on the plantation, but his mind was on Dolley. He asked her cousin Catherine Coles, who lived near Hanover, to tell Dolley how much he loved her. Catherine wrote Dolley: "He thinks so much of you in the Day that he has Lost his Tongue. At Night he dreams of you."

In August, Dolley, with Anna and Payne, headed for Harewood, where her sister Lucy and her mother eagerly awaited her visit. On the way, she stopped overnight at an inn in Fredericksburg and wrote Madison the letter he had anxiously awaited. She accepted his proposal and invited him to meet her at Lucy's. The groom-to-be was ecstatic. He wrote back on August 18, 1794: "I cannot express . . . the joy it gave me . . . I hope you will never have another deliberation on that subject."

Dolley's family welcomed James Madison to Harewood. As soon as the prospective groom found a moment alone with Dolley, he slipped a gold ring set with a cluster of eight rose diamonds on her finger and urged her to marry him at once. Again Dolley hesitated,

James Madison made his home at Montpelier, his Virgina plantation.
(Courtesy of the Library of Congress.)

but her deepening feelings and growing appreciation for Madison as a husband and father to Payne encouraged her to set the date for September 15, barely four months after their formal introduction, and six weeks before the first year of her widowhood ended.

Lucy insisted that Harewood was the ideal place for the wedding. The beautiful blue-gray limestone mansion had a staircase similar to the one at George Washington's Mount Vernon, but wider. The elegant drawing room had walls covered in watered silk and a mantel of green marble—a startling contrast to the stark

Meeting House in Philadelphia, where she had married John Todd.

A state of excitement engulfed the household. Dolley had little time to prepare. She decided on a small family wedding and sent invitations to Madison's sister Nelly and her husband, Major Isaac Hite, who lived nearby. There would not be time for people who lived farther away to get there.

On her wedding day, Dolley stole away from her family to write to Eliza. On this day she was marrying "the man . . . I most admire . . . and my little Payne will have a generous and kind protector."

Dolley's low-cut wedding gown of white satin was daintily patterned with lace and tightly cinched at the waist. She wore white satin low-heeled shoes so she would not tower over the groom, and a wreath of white flowers crowned her hair. Clasped about her neck, for all to see, was Madison's wedding gift—a mosaic necklace depicting subjects from Roman history.

A radiant Dolley descended the staircase and took her place beside James Madison. Following the Episcopalian ceremony, the wedding party celebrated with a festive supper. A tinkling harpsichord added a light-hearted touch, and accompanied by fiddlers, the guests joined together and sang songs such as "Possum in de Gum Tree." The usually sedate, collected groom let the young Payne girls cut the fine Mechlin lace ruffles off his shirt for keepsakes.

Dolley was now married to one of the most admired men in the United States. She would have a position of respect and prestige, and she admired Madison deeply. But her first husband, whom she had loved, had been dead for only a year. It was a day of mixed feelings that she summarized in a postscript to the letter she had written to Eliza earlier in the day: "Evening. Dolley Madison! Alas!"

Chapter Five

Mrs. James Madison

James and Dolley Madison spent the first few days of their honeymoon in a cozy, one-room stone cottage on the estate at Harewood. The cabin was secluded, but it offered the newlyweds little privacy because young Payne continued to sleep with his mother every night. Madison hoped for some time alone with Dolley when he arranged to break their stay at Harewood with a visit to Belle Grove, the nearby home of his sister Nelly Hite. It was not to be. Payne, who could have stayed with his grandmother, went along, as did Anna and Harriet Washington, sister of George Steptoe.

Dolley felt at home at Belle Grove. She walked in the gardens and played with Payne and the Hite children. She wanted to learn more about her husband's childhood and education, and talkative Nelly shared stories about her favorite brother.

James, a child of the Virginia planter aristocracy, was the oldest of ten children, of which only five survived infancy. Unlike his brothers, he had little interest in farming. He liked books, and his father saw to it that he had the best possible education. At age eighteen, he set out on horseback from the family home at Montpelier to New Jersey to attend college. At what is now known as Princeton University, James studied law, government, philosophy, languages, and astronomy. Sleeping no more than five hours each night, he graduated in two years. Nelly claimed that the spirited discussions and debates at Princeton spawned Madison's ideas on how governments should work.

James Madison and Isaac Hite talked often about the triumphs and troubles facing the new nation. Great Britain seized food from American ships bound for France and forced American sailors to join the Royal Navy. They wondered if the envoy to England, John Jay, would be able to successfully work out a treaty protecting American rights on the high seas.

Soon, the leisurely honeymoon days at the Hites' ended and the Madisons returned to Harewood. Dolley became ill—a slight relapse of the fever she had suffered in August. In a letter to his father dated October 5, 1794, James wrote, "In about 8 or 10 days we expect to set out for Philadelphia, and your daughter-in-law begs you and my mother to accept her best and most respectable affections, which she means to express herself by an early opportunity."

The Harewood family waved goodbye as the fancy new coach carrying Mr. and Mrs. Madison, Payne, and Anna headed north. They crossed the Potomac at Harper's

Ferry. A riot of fall colors graced the roadside, but deep ruts, dust, mud, mountain slopes, and rocky streambeds made the going exhausting and dangerous. The new carriage shook so much that it almost fell apart. James Madison had to resort to tying broken pieces of the carriage together. They rattled into Philadelphia in mid-October 1794, just in time for the new session of Congress.

The Madisons moved into the house that had been left vacant by the recent departure of James Monroe, who was now appointed the U.S. minister to France. They furnished their rented home with pieces from Montpelier and a few new purchases. While Madison went about the business of Congress, Dolley began to learn about the world of politics. Prior to her marriage to James Madison, Dolley had not moved in political circles.

Marriage congratulations poured in from friends and colleagues. Thomas Jefferson feared that James Madison might retire from public life now that he was married, instead of taking on "a more splendid . . . and officious post." The post he referred to was the presidency of the United States. Jefferson wrote from Monticello, "Present me respectably to Mrs. Madison, and pray her to keep you where you are for your own satisfaction and the public good."

On December 2, Dolley received the anticipated news that her life-long membership in the Society of Friends had ended because of her marriage to a non-Quaker. She may have been relieved. According to one ob-

A constant friend to the Madisons, President Thomas Jefferson would be instrumental
in furthering James's political career. *(Courtesy of the Library of Congress.)*

server, she always was "an odd bird in a Quaker nest."

Dolley blossomed as Mrs. James Madison. She relished wearing silks, satins, and brocades that had so long been denied her. Dolley stood out among the stylishly dressed women of Philadelphia because of her talent for choosing clothes that suited her best. This did not happen by chance. Her study of beautiful women that began as a wide-eyed fifteen-year-old continued. "I went yesterday to see a doll," she wrote, "dressed to show us the fashions, and I saw besides a great quantity of millinery." Shoes were Dolley's greatest extravagance. Though it may have strained James's budget, Dolley often bought twenty pairs at a time.

Dolley maintained her independent spirit. She balked at the fashionable practice of wearing a wig. Although the president and Mrs. Washington never appeared in public without a wig, she chose to show off her thick dark hair. Other women—in Philadelphia, New York, Boston, and Charleston—took note and followed her example. By 1797, it had become old-fashioned to powder one's hair or wear a wig. This was Dolley's first impact on the fashion world.

Dolley adapted quickly to the social life of Philadelphia. At the time of her marriage to Madison, she had never attended a dinner party or reception, much less a ball. Now she plunged into these festivities with such zeal that it was hard to imagine that she had known any other life. Each week her bright personality enlivened Martha Washington's somewhat stuffy Friday afternoon social gatherings.

Amid the excitement of her new social life, Dolley remained close to her family. She launched her sister Anna into Philadelphia society and frequently invited Mary to come up from the country to visit. In January 1795, Dolley learned that her brothers William and Isaac had died. Both had been shot in separate incidents. Her oldest brother, Walter, sailed to England in 1785 and vanished from the family records. John was her only remaining brother. Little Payne turned three in February 1795. He romped with his "Papa" and was spoiled by everyone. James also fulfilled the role of father to sixteen-year-old Anna.

As Congress made preparations to adjourn in March 1795, the entire country awaited the outcome of John Jay's mission to England. At the time of adjournment, the terms of the treaty that would hopefully protect American ships remained secret. There was nothing to do but wait.

Six months after his marriage, Madison set off with his little family to introduce them to the rest of the Madisons at Montpelier. Before they were married, Madison had assured Dolley that his family "will love you as I do, beloved." He was right.

Jay returned from Europe, and President Washington summoned the Senate to a special session on June 8 to ratify the Jay Treaty. Though the president tried to keep the document secret until it was formally presented to the Senate, its contents leaked out. When he learned the terms of the treaty, James Madison was upset. He thought it was a disaster for the United States. England agreed to evacuate forts in the Northwest. However, there was not one word in the document about the capture of American ships and the forcing of American seamen into the British navy. Restrictions were placed on American trade. He argued that the Jay Treaty restricted the sovereign freedom of the United States. Many others agreed; there was a great outcry against the treaty. Riots broke out and John Jay was burned in effigy. When Alexander Hamilton attempted to defend the Jay Treaty at an outdoor meeting in New York, angry protestors threw stones at him.

When the Madisons returned to Philadelphia in the fall, they moved into a three-story brick house at 4295 Spruce Street. James was more deeply embroiled than ever in what his wife called "public business." Wherever they went, they heard people discussing the Jay Treaty. The Madisons invited people of differing opinions to dinner parties in their own home. Abigail Adams, wife of Vice President John Adams, stated that everyone prized an invitation to dine with Mrs. Madison.

Dolley learned a great deal about politics at these social gatherings. During Washington's second term in office, two political parties emerged. Each party had different ideas about the new government. The Federalists, led by Alexander Hamilton, the first secretary of the treasury, believed in a strong central government. Thomas Jefferson and James Madison headed the Democratic-Republicans, commonly called the Republicans. They believed in less governmental control and more individual liberties. The Republican Party eventually

Alexander Hamilton believed the new country should be led by a strong federal government. *(Courtesy of the Library of Congress.)*

changed its name and is the forerunner of today's Democratic Party. Dolley made sure that every social event in the Madison home included both Federalists and Republicans.

In 1796, in addition to her growing reputation as a charming hostess, Dolley became the undisputed fashion leader of America. She loved the latest French styles then crossing the Atlantic and caused a sensation when she appeared at a ball wearing an imported, high-waisted, gray satin dress with short sleeves and a revealing neckline. She wore two sweeping plumes in her dark hair. Most American women had shied away from the latest fashions, but the following day the dressmakers of Philadelphia were swamped with orders for copies of her dress. Years later, Dolley donned the same style gown when she sat for her portrait by Gilbert Stuart.

James Madison enjoyed the stir his wife created. Even though he had overcome some of his shyness in social situations, he could usually be found in a corner during a party, quietly conferring with other congressmen and foreign dignitaries. After the Republicans lost the vote to kill the Jay Treaty in the spring of 1796, a frustrated James considered retiring from politics.

President Washington waited until September to announce that he would not seek a third term (presidents were not limited to two terms of office at this time). In November, Federalist John Adams was elected president of the United States. Republican Thomas Jefferson came in second in the balloting, which made him vice president.

The election results strengthened James's desire to retire, and he announced that he and his family would be returning to Virginia after the new president and vice president were sworn into office. Although Dolley loved the brisk social life of Philadelphia, she would have to return to Virginia with her husband.

Chapter Six

"Within a Squirrel's Jump of Heaven"

On March 4, 1797, Dolley and James Madison attended the inauguration of John Adams. It was their last public appearance before leaving for Montpelier. Adams stood before the assembled crowd in his plain, gray suit, but all eyes were on a tall, familiar figure clad in a black velvet suit, dress sword hanging by his side. Many shed tears as George Washington, their wartime and peacetime leader for twenty years, bowed a silent farewell. This was Dolley's last sight of the first president.

As George and Martha Washington headed to Mount Vernon in a cream colored coach, the Madisons packed. After twenty-one years of public service, James Madison had decided to abandon politics. Moving turned out to be quite an undertaking. They shipped five bushels of clover seed, eighteen chairs, and sixteen pieces of luggage by water. Extra horses and wagons came up from the Virginia plantation to haul furniture and other personal belongings.

In the spring of 1797, Dolley climbed into the carriage with her husband, Payne, and Anna. After the glamour and excitement of being in the national limelight, she would be living the quiet life of a farmer's wife. She had plenty of time to think during the leisurely roundabout journey to Montpelier. They traveled for six weeks through Harper's Ferry, Warm Springs, and Harewood, where they had been married two and a half years before.

The Madisons reached Montpelier in time to see the dogwoods at their loveliest. The brick house sat on a hill facing the hazy Blue Ridge Mountains, as Dolley said, "within a squirrel's jump of Heaven."

Dolley and James settled into plantation life. James took over management of the plantation from his aging father. He abhorred slavery, but he had long ago given up the idea that he could manage without his one hundred slaves. Although he had not liked farming as a boy, he now plunged into running the farm, experimenting with crop rotation and fertilizers. The scholar-turned-farmer almost doubled the plantation's profits within the first year.

James Madison enlarged the main house at Montpelier to make it more comfortable for two families. Dolley took care of the furnishings while James superintended the renovations. Acting as his own architect, James added wings and a sixty-foot portico with white pillars to the eight-room square house. He purchased fifty thousand handmade nails from Jefferson's Monticello factory. He ordered 190 French window panes from a factory in Philadelphia. The noise of hammers and saws filled the air in the spring of 1798. Workmen mixed mortar and trundled wheelbarrows.

Dolley loved Montpelier and immersed herself in the task of running a two-household family. She had the blessing of her mother-in-law, Nellie. The two developed a close relationship. Dolley planned meals, worked in the gardens, and supervised the cleaning and maintenance of the house. She directed the making of new clothes, even sewing many garments herself, and assumed the role of hostess at the estate, transforming Montpelier into a center of country social life. Friends and relatives visited frequently. Because travel was slow and difficult, visitors from far away tended to stay for several days or weeks.

Dolley continued to overindulge Payne. The broad lawns were a perfect place for her son to run and explore the outdoors. He began to show more willfulness, but in his mother's eyes, Payne could do no wrong. Like Dolley, James, who accepted Payne as his own, never refused him anything.

When James Monroe returned from his post as minister to France, he built a home only a short distance from Montpelier. As was the custom among diplomats, the Monroes brought French goods to be offered for sale to their friends. A wagon sent from Montpelier picked up "two tablecloths large enough for an eighteen-foot table plus . . . four dozen used but serviceable napkins." The purchase of secondhand articles from the Monroes began a pattern of buying secondhand goods that the Madisons would use until the end of their lives.

The two families often exchanged dinner visits. Both men liked to walk. After a meal, they would go for long walks, leaving Dolley and Elizabeth Monroe to chat. As busy as he was with farm duties, James had not forgotten politics.

Because of their husbands' close political ties, the wives spent many hours together. But as far as it is known, they never called each other by their first names. They were never close. Elizabeth Monroe was from a prominent New York family and had traveled and lived in Europe. However, she had little interest in clothes or food and regarded entertaining as a chore.

The Madisons often exchanged visits with neighbor Thomas Jefferson. Montpelier and Monticello were thirty miles apart—a day's journey. At Monticello, the room kept for James and Dolley's use was known as the "Madison chamber." Dolley enjoyed the company of Jefferson's daughter Martha Randolph who lived at Monticello with her growing family. Dolley was fascinated by Jefferson's many inventions—the dumbwaiter that brought wines from the basement to the dining room, folding ladder, swivel chair, and the clock showing the days of the week. While Dolley visited with the Randolphs, Jefferson and James Madison discussed cattle and tobacco prices, and plots by the Federalists to destroy the Republican Party.

Madison had concerns over the fate of the nation. He blamed the XYZ Affair—the name given to France's outrageous demands to the United States—on the Jay

Treaty. Though war was never declared, the XYZ incident led to fighting at sea between France and the United States.

More alarming news reached Montpelier. The Federalists had passed the Alien and Sedition Acts. The acts made it difficult for foreigners to become citizens of the United States and undercut freedom of the press. Madison and Jefferson viewed the acts as a direct attack on the Bill of Rights and worked out a plan to present anonymous resolutions in various state legislatures to declare the acts unconstitutional. Virginia and Kentucky passed these resolutions, but other states refused to do so. The situation became so tense that friends pressured James Madison to run for election to the Virginia Assembly. One wrote, "If you will not save yourself or your friends—yet save your country." Madison agreed to run.

In the spring of 1799, the Madisons hosted a wedding at Montpelier. Dolley's youngest sister, Mary, married Congressman J.G. Jackson. Dolley's mother, young John, Lucy, and George Steptoe drove over from Harewood for the happy occasion.

That summer, four Doric columns were erected on Montpelier's sixty-foot porch. After Madison's carpenters failed to hoist the pillars into position, a skilled stonecutter arrived from Thomas Jefferson's Monticello and finished the job. When it rained, Dolley and James took exercise by running races on the porch. James would check his tin measuring cup to see how many inches of rain had fallen on his fields.

Madison easily won election to the General Assembly. From 1799 to 1800, he served in the Virginia legislature in Richmond. In December 1799, George Washington died at his Mount Vernon estate. The Madisons, along with other prominent Virginians, and scores from other states, traveled to Mount Vernon to pay their last respects. The usually composed Dolley wept in public. In a letter to Lucy, Dolley wrote that her grief and her husband's were so great that "we exchanged scarce a word on our sad journey home."

As the presidential election year of 1800 approached, the country was in a state of turmoil. Because of the threatening international situation and the attempts to curtail civil liberties, public opinion had turned against President Adams and the Federalists. All signs pointed to a victory for the Republicans. In the election, Thomas Jefferson and Aaron Burr competed against John Adams and Charles Cotesworth Pinckney—nominees of the Federalist Party. It was the first bitterly fought presidential election; both sides were guilty of smear tactics. The Republicans won in the December election; however, Jefferson and Burr had tied. Under these circumstances, the delegates in the House of Representatives, now representing sixteen states, had to decide who would become president.

At Montpelier, Dolley and James anxiously awaited news of the balloting. For almost a week, there was a deadlock. Finally, after thirty-six ballots, Jefferson received the necessary two-thirds of the vote. In mid-February 1801, a galloping messenger delivered a handbill to Montpelier. Dolley listened as James read aloud: "Ten for Jefferson. I hope you will have the cannon out." Dolley knew that this meant the end of James's retirement. Soon, she would be packing again.

Chapter Seven

Washington City Hostess

President Jefferson asked Madison to be secretary of state. Although he had intended to retire from politics, Madison knew he could not refuse the request. He was convinced that the Federalists had damaged U.S. foreign policy. On February 27, 1801, Dolley and James were packing for the move to the nation's new capital city on the banks of the Potomac when seventy-seven-year-old James Madison Sr. died. James wrote to Thomas Jefferson, "Yesterday morning rather suddenly though very gently, the flame of life went out."

With moving plans on hold, Dolley attended to the needs of her mother-in-law and greeted family members and the hundreds who came to the estate to pay their respects. James had to settle the large and complex estate. His part of the estate totaled about five thousand acres and the Montpelier mansion. His mother would continue to occupy the south wing and to maintain a private staff.

On March 4, 1801, plainly dressed Thomas Jefferson strolled to the Capitol to take the oath of office as the third president of the United States. Still detained by family affairs, James and Dolley were not present to hear their friend's inaugural speech: "Let us then, fellow citizens, unite with one heart and one mind; let us restore . . . harmony and affection . . . We are all Republicans, we are all Federalists." John Adams also missed the address. The ex-president's coach had rattled out of town before dawn.

The following day, Jefferson officially announced his cabinet appointments. No one was surprised to learn that James Madison would be secretary of state. A week later, Jefferson, on his way to Monticello for a brief visit, stopped overnight at Montpelier. He arrived alone on horseback, determined to make good on his promise to rid the office of anything resembling royalty.

After dinner, the two men exchanged ideas regarding the direction of the new administration. They were both angry that John Adams had appointed federal judges, dubbed "midnight judges," at the last minute of his presidency. James accepted the invitation to live with the president until the Madisons found suitable lodging.

On the first day of May 1801, after navigating the muddy roads between Montpelier and Washington City, the Madison family jolted down the pothole filled Pennsylvania Avenue in their dusty carriage. The carriage stopped in front of the building referred to simply as the "President's House" (later it would be called the

This plan of the city of Washington was created in 1792. When the Madisons arrived in 1801, however, the "President's House" was not yet completed. *(Courtesy of the Library of Congress.)*

White House). The weary occupants—James, Dolley, Payne, and Anna—dismounted and entered the gray stone mansion.

The half-finished house, surrounded by mounds of stones and bricks, looked more like a ruin than a new building. Abigail Adams, the first presidential spouse to live in the President's House, found the building to be damp and drafty. She expressed her frustrations in a letter to her daughter: "If they will put me up some bells, and let me have wood enough to keep fires . . . I

could content myself almost anywhere for three months
. . . and the great unfinished audience room I make a
drying-room of, to hang up the wash in." Mrs. Adams
was happy to leave the President's House.

On May 2, 1801, James Madison took the oath of
office as secretary of state. Dolley house hunted while
Madison put in long hours on his new job. Washington
City, as it was called then, had been ten years in the
making. However, buildings were few and forests and
wildlife abounded. One and a half miles of swampland
separated the President's House from the Capitol. After
three weeks of searching, Dolley found a small house to
rent on M Street. Jefferson would gladly have shared
the presidential mansion with the Madison family in-
definitely—but the Federalists had joked that the president was "taking boarders."

Most government officials left Washington City during the muggy summer months. The Madisons headed
to Montpelier following the Fourth of July celebration.
After the summer vacation, they moved into a large new
house on F Street, two blocks east of the executive
mansion. Next-door neighbor, Dr. William Thornton,
had arranged for them to lease the house.

During the fall of 1801, thirty-three-year-old Dolley
plunged into a whirl of social activity. In the F Street
house, with its reception room, large drawing room, and
dining facilities, Dolley enthusiastically threw herself
into Washington society. She knew that social affairs
could be used for political purposes and invitations to
events at the Madisons were highly prized. Congress-

While James was secretary of state, the Madison's lived in a rowhouse at 1333 F Street.
(Courtesy of the Library of Congress.)

men, heads of departments, foreign ministers, report-
ers, friends, Republicans, and Federalists wanted to be
guests of the Madisons. At the time, one reporter wrote,
"It would be hard to overestimate the social influence
of Mrs. Madison." Soon Dolley Madison was the
capital's premier hostess.

Determined to strip away the formality of previous
administrations, Jefferson announced that he would hold
public receptions only twice a year—New Year's Day
and the Fourth of July. Because Jefferson and Vice
President Burr were both widowers, Dolley or another
lady acted as hostess on special occasions. Jefferson's
primary entertaining strategy was to have a series of
small dinner parties that consisted of men of one congressional party or the other seated at a round table.

Jefferson's informality led to some clumsy bumbling, especially when the first minister to the United States from Great Britain, Anthony Merry, came to visit. James Madison accompanied Minister Merry to the President's House to be formally presented. According to Merry, the president was "not merely in an undress, but *actually standing in slippers down at the heels*, and both pantaloons, coat, and underclothes indicative of slovenliness." During the interview, Jefferson idly tossed one of his slippers in the air, catching it with his big toe.

Three days later, the British minister and his wife, Elizabeth, arrived at the president's door to what they assumed was a dinner in their honor. When dinner was announced, Jefferson took the arm of the lady next to him—Mrs. Madison. Aware of the correct protocol, Dolley whispered to him, "Take Mrs. Merry." Jefferson, however, proceeded to escort Dolley into dinner, to the horror of the stunned guests. James Madison rushed to take Mrs. Merry to the table and sat down beside her, leaving the dazed minister to scrounge for a seat. Merry reported to his government that he had been snubbed. James tried to soothe the furious British diplomat by explaining that the president believed that etiquette had no place in a republic. But the damage had been done, and the Merrys refused to dine with the president again.

Jefferson and the Republicans were strongly anti-British and had aligned themselves with the French in the war that was wracking Europe. The Federalists supported the British. This conflict played itself out in many ways, not least of which was a "press war" between rival newspapers. It was this aspect of the conflict that had motivated the Federalists to support the Sedition Act. Now that the Republicans were in power, their press supporters harrassed the British ambassador and his noble wife. Elizabeth Merry was determined to fulfill her social duties, in spite of the abuse she suffered in the newspapers and sometimes in public. When she attended a party in Georgetown to mark the Senate's ratification of the Louisiana Purchase, which doubled the size of the United States, Mrs. Merry was told at the door that her "undemocratic diamonds" had to be removed before she could enter. This type of offense was even too much for Jefferson, and the etiquette war finally fizzled out. But it did little to lessen the tensions between the two parties. In the following years, Dolley Madison worked to define a social style for the new republic.

Esteemed portrait painter Gilbert Stuart spent the winter of 1803 in Washington City. He was all the rage and both Dolley and James sat for portraits that became favorites among the many of Stuarts that were preserved. Stuart also painted Dolley's sister Anna Payne. During one of her sittings, Anna requested a portrait of Stuart. A close look at Anna's portrait reveals a self-caricature of the great artist in the background drapery.

Anna, charming, poised, and as elegant as Dolley, had many admirers. Her engagement to wealthy, Harvard educated Congressman Richard Cutts of Massachusetts was bittersweet news for Dolley. The wedding festivities—Washington City's most important social event of the spring of 1804—took place at the Madison home. After the newlyweds departed for Cutts's home, Dolley expressed her loneliness to a friend. "One of the greatest griefs of my life has come to me in the parting for the first time from my sister-child."

To ease the pain of separation, Dolley corresponded with Anna. In a letter dated April 26, 1804, Dolley Madison related the sad news of the death of Jefferson's daughter Maria Eppes, who was twenty-five, the same age as Anna. "This is among the many proofs, my dear sister, of the uncertainty of life." Dolley's letter of July 16, 1804, includes one sentence about another shocking event, "You have no doubt heard of the terrible duel, and death of poor Hamilton."

Vice President Aaron Burr harbored a list of resentments against former Secretary of Treasury Alexander Hamilton. Both men were from New York, and both burned with ambition. Burr blamed Hamilton for his loss in the 1800 presidential election and his loss in the 1804 race for governor of New York. When Burr received word that Hamilton had insulted him publicly, he challenged him to a duel. Burr may have thought the challenge would boost his sagging political career.

The two longtime personal and political enemies met on the dueling grounds at Weehawken, New Jersey, at dawn on July 11, 1804. Each fired a shot. Burr remained unscathed but Hamilton fell to the ground. "This is a mortal wound, Doctor," Hamilton uttered to the attending physician. Then he lapsed into unconscious-

Alexander Hamilton was mortally wounded in a duel with Aaron Burr.
(Courtesy of the Library of Congress.)

ness and died the next day. Witnesses later claimed that Hamilton had fired intentionally into the air.

Instead of reviving Burr's political carccr, thc ducl ended it. Aaron Burr became a renegade after his term of vice president ended. At no time did Dolley reveal her personal feelings about the matter, although Burr was a family friend who had boarded in the Payne house in Philadelphia and had introduced her to James Madison.

In spite of another bruising campaign, Jefferson was reelected president in November, with aging George Clinton of New York serving as vice president. This meant another four years in the house on F Street for the Madisons. Dolley served as hostess at Jefferson's second inauguration reception on March 5, 1805. A French diplomat wrote of the event in a letter to Paris: "Mrs. Madison has become one of America's most valuable assets. She would be equally at ease in any of the world's capitals."

That summer, Dolley developed a knee infection. She wrote to Anna that she had attended Jefferson's July 4 reception, "sitting still, and amusing myself with the mob." When Dolley's knee did not improve, Madison insisted that a professor from the University of Pennsylvania, Dr. Physick, treat her. Instead of their usual summer trek to Montpelier, the Madisons set out for Philadelphia, leaving Dolley's mother in charge of fifteen-year-old Payne.

Upon their arrival, they went straight to the doctor. The report was good—no surgery or amputation. Dolley reported to Anna: "We are in excellent lodgings on Sansom Street . . . Dr. Physick has put my knee in splints, and promises me a cure in time." With her leg sticking straight out from the hip, Dolley had plenty of time to rest. Visitors streamed through her bedroom while Madison kept busy with his correspondence.

For three months, James Madison watched over his wife. He left the nation's problems to others and the tobacco crop drying at Montpelier to his overseer. But, because of alarming developments abroad, Jefferson summoned James Madison back to Washington City in October. He returned alone. During the month-long separation, Dolley wrote James every day. The surviving letters reveal the deep love Dolley felt for her husband. He was barely out of sight before she began writing, "I find nothing can relieve the oppression of my mind but speaking to you, in this, the only way." Another letter ended with, "Adieu, my beloved, our hearts understand each other." On another occasion she wrote: "My darling husband . . . To find you love me, have my child safe, and that my mother is well, seems to comprise all my happiness."

As soon as Dolley was able to ride, she took care of some business pertaining to the house she owned in Philadelphia, bought a pair of carriage horses for Madison, and shopped. The president had asked her to buy the latest fashions for his daughter Martha Randolph. She did so by having the shop clerks bring articles out to the carriage for her approval. The night before her departure for Washington City, Dolley gave a reception for her many Philadelphia friends. Anna and her husband, Richard Cutts, joined Dolley on the journey to the capital. A fully recovered Dolley returned to F Street four months after she had left in misery.

The winter after Dolley's return from Philadelphia turned out to be an unusually brilliant social season in the capital. Jefferson's daughter Martha came to Washington City for the winter, bringing her five daughters and one son. Martha presided as hostess at her father's New Year's Day reception and at other social functions, although she did have to take time off from her social duties to give birth to another son. Named James Madison, he was the first person born in the White House.

As if to make up for the months as an invalid, Dolley gave larger parties than ever in the F Street house. Like Jefferson, she often served ice cream wrapped in warm pastry at dinner parties. After dinner, card tables were set up and guests gambled, if they so desired. One guest, referring to the crowds at the Madisons, wrote, "they are worshipping the rising sun." It was obvious that Thomas Jefferson was grooming James Madison to be the next president.

In 1806, some unusual visitors converged on the capital. Tunisian ambassador Sidi Suliman Mellimelli hoped to persuade Jefferson to pay a bounty to Tunisia to protect American ships from pirates. Jefferson refused what he considered to be blackmail. However, Mellimelli and his entourage, including an interpreter, an Italian band, and the carrier of his four-foot pipe, added zest to social gatherings. Black-bearded, white-turbaned Mellimelli, attired in scarlet and gold silks, cut an impressive figure. The Washington ladies crowded around wherever he went. He entertained the curious women—including Dolley—by unwinding and rewinding his twenty-yard muslin turban.

At one of Dolley's receptions, Mellimelli spied a servant coming from the kitchen with a platter of cakes. The delighted Tunisian threw his arms around the startled girl, exclaiming in Turkish: "You are the handsomest woman in America! You look like one of my wives, the high priced one—a load for a camel." Washingtonians roared with laughter upon hearing the translation.

Delegations of Native Americans—Osage, Pawnee,

Missouri, Creek—arrived for treaty talks with the president and the secretary of state. Dolley gave a number of receptions and dinner parties at which the guest list included the Native American delegations, congressmen, and foreign ministers. She devoted time to each guest, regardless of nationality or position. She acted graciously when one of the Osage delegates ate with his hands instead of her flatware. It is not known how many Native Americans came to Washington City at this time, but Dolley's social register listed ninety-one.

Amidst the excitement of the social activities, Dolley kept up with all the political turmoil facing the nation—from growing tensions with Native Americans in the western states to continued attacks on American ships by the warring nations of Great Britain and France. While recuperating in Philadelphia, she had asked Madison to "indulge me with some information respecting the disagreement with England . . . I am extremely anxious to hear."

In the autumn of 1807, Dolley's mother died. By the time the news reached the capital, the body of Mary Payne was buried. To add to the gloom, Dolley's sister Mary was dying of tuberculosis.

Hoping to prevent war, Congress passed the Embargo Act in mid-December of 1807. This law prohibited all ships from entering or leaving American ports. This effort to use economic sanctions as a foreign policy tool failed. Merchants in New England suffered because of the inability to do business with foreign nations and many turned to smuggling. Southern farmers lost markets for their goods and American sailors found themselves without income and their ships rotting at the wharves.

As economic disaster loomed, public sentiment turned against the administration. When Madison was nominated as the Republican candidate for president, the Federalists mounted a smear campaign that included gossip about the morals of Dolley and her sister Anna. If the Madisons were disturbed by this abuse, they did not show it. James encouraged Dolley to continue her entertaining "regardless of dirty politics."

The election was held in November 1808, and in February 1809, Congress announced the electoral count. Despite the tactics of the opposition, James Madison won easily. A month before Madison took office, Congress canceled the Embargo Act and replaced it with a new law that allowed trade with all nations except Britain and France. It did little to lessen the tensions. War seemed inevitable, and no one knew better than Madison himself the dire international situation he was inheriting. Having served as secretary of state for eight years, Madison felt prepared for the job.

Chapter Eight

Becoming First Lady

James Madison's presidential inauguration on March 4, 1809, marked the beginning of a new administration and a new role for Dolley Madison. After the noon ceremony at the Capitol, cannons boomed a salute to the fourth president, bands played, and more than ten thousand people lined the streets—cheering, waving handkerchiefs, and tossing hats.

An open house at the Madison home on F Street followed the parade. Guests, having waited for more than an hour to get in, found the entry, parlors, and bedrooms packed with well wishers. Margaret Bayard Smith, wife of the editor of the *National Intelligence*, recorded that Dolley looked "extremely beautiful" dressed in a "plain cambric dress with a very long train . . . and beautiful bonnet of purple velvet and white satin with white plumes. She was all dignity, grace, and affability." Dignified James Madison may have felt he was bowing to every man and woman in the country— but there was more to come.

That evening, the first inaugural ball ever held in Washington honored James Madison, the fourth president. Modest by today's standards, it was elegant for the time. Candlelight blazed from the windows of Long's Hotel, the present site of the Library of Congress, and sounds of violins greeted the Madisons as they arrived in a new state carriage.

More than four hundred people came from near and far. Former President Jefferson attended the ball. It had been forty years since Jefferson, described as being in high spirits and beaming with joy, had been to a dance. Guests craned to see Dolley's handsome son, seventeen-year-old Payne, who was home from boarding school for the occasion.

Beautiful women attired in elaborate gowns crowded into the ballroom and pretty girls tried out new dance steps. However, no one attracted more attention than the president's wife. Mrs. Smith reported that Dolley "looked a queen. She had on a pale buff colored velvet, made plain, with a very long train, but not the least trimming, and beautiful pearl necklace, earrings, and bracelets. Her headdress was a turban of the same coloured velvet and white satin (from Paris) with two superb plumes, the bird of paradise feathers." Dolley's face was as luminous as her pearls, a celebration present from her husband.

Dolley was "almost pressed to death" by the "moving mass" that peered over shoulders to catch a glimpse of the new president's wife. High up, above everyone's head, were two swaying and nodding birds of paradise. In the midst of the festivities, sounds of crashing glass

James Madison served as the nation's president from 1809 to 1817.
(Courtesy of the Library of Congress.)

filled the room. The stale air in the hall had become so unbearable that windows had to be smashed to let in fresh air. Dolley relished every moment of the evening, laughing and chatting. However, her watchful eye noted her exhausted husband and they left two hours early.

A week later, Jefferson headed back to the Virginia hills. On March 11, James and Dolley Madison moved into the nearly empty official residence on Pennsylvania Avenue. Just as Madison knew full well the enormous burdens resting on his shoulders, Dolley, more than any president's wife before or since, stepped into a recognized position.

Before the inauguration, Dolley began making plans for renovating and decorating the executive mansion. James Madison turned the whole project over to her, an unusual decision for that time. Because great homes were status symbols, men usually chose the wallpaper, paint, fabrics, furniture, and even china patterns. Dolley enlisted the help of noted architect Benjamin Latrobe. In order to gain support for the project, she took members of Congress on a tour of the rundown mansion. Proclaiming the official residence a national disgrace, Congress appropriated funds for the renovations.

Dolley's taste in furniture had changed over the years. After her marriage to Madison, she grew to love French furniture as well as French clothes. She had decorated the F Street house and Montpelier with French furnishings. However, French furniture was out of the question for the President's House. The mansion had to celebrate American artisans as well as impress foreign diplomats.

Dolley concentrated on decorating the President's House (right) with a distinctively American flair. *(Courtesy of the Library of Congress.)*

Dolley and Latrobe focused on creating large public rooms suitable for entertaining. They filled the rooms with beautiful American-crafted furniture. Although none of the original furnishings remain, written accounts describe them as elegant. Dolley's genius lay not only in her taste but also in her skill of using Republican simplicity and Federalist high style in a way that received compliments from American and European visitors alike. Her choices of accessories—fine candles and lamps, silver, carpets, wallpaper, imported drapery and upholstery fabrics, large mirrors, and American art—added elegance. Latrobe spent $3,150 on four pairs of mirrors before the Madisons moved into the house. Most items for the mansion came from the big shops in Philadelphia.

Although the two decorators agreed on most things,

Latrobe was not as fond of bright colors as Dolley. The former Quaker enjoyed the rich colors that had been denied her in her youth. Dolley's selection of red curtains for the drawing room caused Latrobe to cry: "The curtains! Oh the terrible velvet curtains! Their effect will ruin me entirely, so brilliant they will be."

The damask curtains and satin upholstery in the sitting room reflected Dolley's fondness for yellow. One stunned visitor noted that the curtains, topping each window, continued "all around the top of the room." A pianoforte and guitar added to the room's decor. Latrobe's idea to hang the George Washington portrait in the dining room triumphed over Dolley's choice of the drawing room. Dolley hung her own portrait in the drawing room.

By the end of May, renovations had progressed enough for Dolley to hold the first of her weekly Wednesday evening "drawing rooms." Dolley was always the star attraction at these functions. Modern scholars of early nineteenth-century political history conclude that Dolley created herself in part through clothing. Today, clothing and jewelry may seem to belong to the frivolous world of fashion, but then they represented different levels of social standing. The two previous presidential wives preferred formal manners and simple dress. Innovative Dolley chose the opposite. She preferred an informal atmosphere, where she dressed like a queen, favoring the French Empire style of dress—cut low in front with short sleeves or no sleeves. Elaborate turbans of silk and satin decorated with feathers and flowers, leaving a few black curls peeping out, became her trademark. One observer, a young bride from North Carolina, noted that the plumes of her turban "distinctly pointed out her station wherever she moved." Reserving white for state occasions, she chose to dress in richly colored, lush fabrics, accented with ermine, lace, or other fine trimmings at her drawing rooms. Women everywhere copied Dolley's style of dress.

Open to everyone, Dolley's Wednesday drawing rooms were more than a place to see or be seen. Attending "Mrs. Madison's crush" provided access to men in power. Two to three hundred people attended the Wednesday night events. There was always the chance that a private word could be had with the busy president. Although Dolley arranged these social occasions to further Madison's political advantage, she never appeared to favor one guest over another. This skill made Dolley a powerful presence in the capital. She would never have considered her role to be the equivalent of the modern first lady—a role that has emerged as an active, political partner of the president. Yet, the politically astute Dolley charmed her husband's enemies and won many supporters—without the hostility heaped upon her predecessor. Strong and intelligent Abigail Adams was called "Madame President" and criticized for being too political. A "lady" of the times did not participate in politics. Until the twentieth century, women, especially wives of presidents, tended to keep a low political profile.

At Dolley's receptions, guests stood and mingled throughout the evening. Unlike the regally seated Martha Washington, Dolley moved from guest to guest. Servants carried huge lacquered trays through the crowd, serving coffee, tea, wines, punch, and light foods as musicians played. On his arrival in the capital, twenty-eight-year old author Washington Irving described emerging "from dirt and darkness into the splendor of Mrs. Madison's drawing room." He found the president's wife "a fine, portly, buxom dame, who has a smile and a pleasant word for everybody." Heedless of her image, Dolley carried around a dainty gold snuff box and invited Madison's political opponents to share a pinch, often breaking the ice between them. On one occasion, she instructed Senator Henry Clay on her method of using snuff. "This is for rough work," she said snorting into a red-checked handkerchief. "And this," she continued, "is my polisher." She daintily applied a fine lace handkerchief to her nose.

At the crowded Wednesday evening receptions, Dolley made a point of greeting everyone. No one introduced to her at one of her parties ever required a second introduction on meeting her again. At one of her gatherings, Dolley noticed a bashful young man backed against a wall. As she maneuvered her way toward him, he accepted a cup of coffee when it passed. Flustered by Dolley's approach, he dropped the saucer onto the floor and tried to stuff the cup into his pocket. Dolley ignored his embarrassment and asked about his family. Soon the boy began to smile—the broken saucer on the floor forgotten.

The Madisons' state dinners were lavish affairs held once a week and included as many as thirty guests. Like Dolley's Wednesday evening drawing rooms, the formal dinners served as an important part of the political process. Republicans and Federalists dined together—unlike Jefferson's dinners. Dolley featured American dishes and sought recipes from all over the country to serve at her formal dinners. Each member of Congress dined at the President's House at least once during each legislative session. Dolley expanded the guest list to include persons of talent in many fields as well as politicians and foreign diplomats. In contrast to Jefferson's use of dumbwaiters, a servant stood behind each guest, providing personal service.

Breaking with custom, Dolley sat at the head of the table, with Madison's secretary Edward Coles at the foot. The president sat in the middle, allowing Dolley to direct the flow of conversation and to spare Madison from this duty. However, James always had a rollicking good story to tell after dessert. Dolley's dinner guests remarked "on the ease with which she glided into the stream of conversation and accommodated herself to its endless variety."

Dolley also hosted parties for women only. At these "dove parties" for cabinet wives, they discussed politics and organized charitable projects that benefited the entire Washington community. To obtain nationwide news firsthand, Dolley organized parties of ladies to attend congressional and Supreme Court sessions. Some men grumbled about women in the galleries, but it did not stop the ladies from attending.

To further political support for her husband, Dolley visited the home of every new congressional family, a physically daunting act. More than just influencing votes, Dolley played a large part in staffing government posts with relatives and friends.

Dolley was well aware of the crisis facing Madison. The conflict with both England and France over freedom on the high seas worsened. He also had to deal with a Congress that Madison called "unhinged." Feeling the weight of his office, Madison slept poorly. Dolley worried about her husband. She kept a large candle burning on his dressing table so that he could read or write in his wakeful hours.

Amid these tensions, Dolley remained calm, keeping up with the endless routine of housekeeping and entertaining. Well trained in both British and French protocol and cuisine, Dolley's butler John Sioussat (Elizabeth Merry's former servant) helped run the domestic and social affairs of the Madison household. Dolley's friendship with Sioussat lasted for many years.

After the furnishing of the President's House was completed, the Madisons invited "houseguests in battalions." Various members of the Madison and Payne families paid long visits. John Quincy Adams, son of President Adams, commented that one of Madison's young nieces or nephews was always underfoot.

In 1810, Lucy Payne Washington, now a widow, moved in with her sister and brother-in-law. She and her three sons remained at the President's House until her marriage to Judge Thomas Todd of Kentucky in 1812.

Planned by Dolley, Lucy's was the first wedding in the presidential mansion.

Summers at Montpelier provided a change from the problems of Washington, although the job pressure never let up. The summer of 1811 held out a ray of hope that relations with England might improve. In May, James Monroe had replaced the inept Robert Smith as secretary of state. The prince regent had recently taken over the English government from his father, George III, who was suffering from an undiagnosed mental illness.

While awaiting news from England—which took six or more weeks—Madison completed the remodeling of Montpelier. In the American History Room, he placed busts of Washington, Adams, and Jefferson. A *bas-relief* (marble carving) of Madison, as well as paintings of patriotic events and portraits of American leaders, hung on the walls.

Guests arrived in droves that summer—some expected, some unexpected. Before dinner, a servant peered through the telescope on the front veranda to see if anyone was driving up the road. Jefferson and Monroe visited. Lucy and Anna and their children stayed for weeks. At one time during the summer, twenty-three children roamed the house. When a friend explained that she did not want to inconvenience Dolley by bringing her little girls, Dolley responded, "I shouldn't have known they were here among all the children."

That summer of 1811 turned out to be a lull before the storm. When the Madisons returned to Washington in October, the president had almost given up hoping that the nation could avoid another war with England.

Chapter Nine

The Burning of Washington

"I believe there will be war," Dolley wrote to her sister Anna. "Mr. Madison sees no end to our perplexities without it." The conflict that had been brewing between the United States and Great Britain since the revolution was leading to war. The primary cause of the war was America's insistence on its right to be neutral in the long conflict between France and Great Britain. Both of the European nations refused to honor U.S. neutrality; Great Britain, still bitter about the loss of the American colonies, refused to stop raiding American shipping. Tensions were also aggravated in the West, where Native Americans were encouraged by the British to raid and harrass white American settlers.

As long as the conflict between Napoleon's French Army and Great Britain consumed Europe, however, war against the United States was avoided. Britain wanted to avoid a "two-front" war. But on June 18, 1812, a few days after Dolley wrote the letter, President Madison signed a declaration of war against Great Britain. He was frustrated by Britain's refusal to stop harrassing American ships, but he was also forced into action by a group of young congressmen, led by Henry Clay of Kentucky and John Calhoun of South Carolina, who were called the "War Hawks." It became politically impossible for the president to avoid open conflict with the British any longer.

Due to the communications time lag, the message did not reach London until two months later. Once again, the nation faced England on its own ground with untrained troops and a seventeen-vessel navy. Britain was the greatest sea power in the world, numbering more than a thousand warships, and its land troops were hardened by years of European war.

The country was divided over how to run the war. Madison's Federalist enemies in the northeast called it "Mr. Madison's War"—in spite of his exhausting efforts to avert a conflict. As a gesture to show that he was commander in chief, Madison wore a little round hat decorated with a cockade (rose-shaped badge) whenever he went out.

As a child, living on an isolated Virginia plantation, Dolley had been unscathed by the Revolutionary War. Twenty-nine years later, with a new war looming, Dolley continued her round of social events and entertaining. She wrote to a friend in Paris: "I will ask the favor of you to send me by safe vessels large headdresses, a few flowers, feathers, gloves and stockings." She considered it her patriotic duty to keep her private and public life as normal as possible.

To add to the Madisons' woes, Payne Todd showed a lack of regard for others that would plague his mother in the future. In the spring of 1812, the handsome six-footer graduated from boarding school. Twenty-two-year-old Payne refused to go on to Princeton. Instead, he made the social rounds of Washington. Girls swarmed the overindulged young man, who wore one of the new green jackets called lizards, with long pointed tails to the calf of the leg and skintight trousers tucked into yellow boots. Payne also spent time betting on the races and playing cards. No amount of persuasion could deter him from his unruly ways. Unknown to Dolley, her husband had secretly been paying Payne's gambling debts for years.

James won reelection to the presidency easily. Some people said that Dolley's popularity with the American people helped her husband win a second term. Clearly Dolley's enormous popularity was a major asset. Prior to the election, Dolley Madison continued to include members of both political parties in her weekly drawing rooms. Twentieth-century writer and president's daughter, Margaret Truman, proclaimed, "Without Dolley, Madison would almost certainly have been a one-term failure."

At first, the War of 1812 went well for the United States. The British were dumbfounded when the *London Times* reported that in seven months the Americans had taken five hundred English merchantmen and three frigates (naval vessels).

Washington society celebrated with a naval ball at

John Payne Todd's gambling debts would plague his mother in later years.
(From The Life and Letters of Dolley Madison *by Allen C. Clark, 1914.)*

Tomlinson's Hotel. A military band played, and as they danced the night away, a young American naval lieutenant carrying a flag burst into the ballroom and announced the surrender of Britain's largest frigate, the *Macedonian,* to Captain Stephen Decatur. The crowd went wild. While the band played "Yankee Doodle," the lieutenant held the *Macedonian's* flag high and paraded around the dance floor. When he came before Dolley, he knelt and laid the captured flag at her feet.

On New Year's Day, 1813, the president's annual reception went on as usual. Guests were still ecstatic over Decatur's naval victory. Dolley looked like a queen in a gown of pink satin trimmed with ermine and gold chains. Two nodding ostrich plumes topped the ever-present turban.

As James entered his second term, Russia offered to negotiate between the United States and Britain. Madison sent two delegates to Russia. An unenthusiastic Payne Todd accompanied the delegates as secretary. His parents thought a year abroad would settle him down. After a few months in cold Russia, playboy Payne slipped off to Paris.

In the summer of 1813, Madison fell ill with malaria. For weeks he lingered between life and death. Dolley nursed him night and day—"as I would an infant," she told a friend. After the fever subsided, Dolley wrote to Madison's secretary, Edward Coles, also ill, in Philadelphia: "Sometimes I despair! But now that I see he will get well, I feel as if I should die myself from fatigue." Within a few days, Dolley showed no ill effects of the ordeal, but the sixty-two-year-old president's recovery was slow.

Madison's illness caused uncertainty in the nation's capital. Acting as substitute secretary, Dolley kept Coles informed of the fears that Washington would be attacked. "The fort is being repaired, and five hundred militia, with perhaps as many regulars, are to be stationed on the Green near the windmill. The twenty tents already look well in my eyes, who have always been an advocate for fighting when assailed though a Quaker. I therefore keep the old Tunisian sabre within reach."

News of a spectacular naval victory reached Madison at Montpelier, where he had gone to recuperate at Dolley's insistence. In September 1813, Captain Oliver Perry captured a British squadron on Lake Erie—two ships, two brigs, one schooner, and one sloop. "We have met the enemy and they are ours," he reported to his commanding general. John Adams commented that this triumph was enough to revive Madison if he were in the last stages of consumption.

Madison returned to Washington to learn that Britain had rejected Russian efforts to work out a peace settlement and had proposed direct negotiations. Washington society continued its carefree existence. However, the president suspected the British were not really interested in peace and called for the defense of Washington. He was hampered from protecting the city by a reluctant cabinet and inept military leaders. Dolley was aware of the impending danger to the nation and to her husband. She told a friend, "In case of an attack . . . I am determined to stay with him." She described the preparation for defense as "constantly retarded."

In mid-August 1814, fifty British warships dropped anchor at the mouth of the Patuxent River, near Chesapeake Bay. Four thousand strong, the troops began a slow march to Washington, intent on burning the city and capturing the president and his wife.

After hearing of the invasion, Madison rode out to army headquarters (nine miles to the east) to inspect preparations for the defense of the capital. What he found was chaos. Orders had not been carried out; roads were not blocked. Up to the actual day of the attack, the secretary of war kept saying that the British planned to attack Baltimore, not Washington.

Before leaving on August 22 to check the defensive front lines at Bladensburg, Maryland, Madison stationed one hundred guards around the mansion and told Dolley to await his return. While Dolley and a few frightened servants remained in the President's House, panic reigned outside. Men left to join the militia and women and children packed their possessions in wagons and carriages and fled.

Outwardly calm, Dolley packed important cabinet papers, as the president had requested. Her pet parrot was taken to the house of the French minister for safekeeping. Just as she had felt compelled to write a letter on her wedding night, she wrote to her sister Lucy a detailed account of the events as they unfolded around her, beginning on Tuesday, August 23, 1814: "Dear Sister—My husband left me yesterday to join General

Winder. He inquired seriously whether I had courage, or firmness to remain in the President's House until his return . . . and on my assurance that I had no fear but for him and the success of our army, he left me, beseeching me to take care of myself and of the cabinet papers, public and private."

That morning, Dolley received two notes from Madison. She told Lucy: "The last is alarming, because he desires I should be ready at a moment's warning to enter my carriage and leave the city; that the enemy seemed stronger than had at first been reported, and it might happen that they would reach the city with the intention of destroying it."

Lack of wagons hampered Dolley's efforts to save the President's House furnishings. However, she yanked down the red velvet drawing room curtains and packed them. Dolley added a few more lines to the letter: "Our private property must be sacrificed . . . I am determined not to go myself until I see Mr. Madison safe and he can accompany me, as I hear of much hostility towards him . . . My friends and acquaintances are all gone."

That evening Madison arrived back at the President's House. Dolley was relieved to see her husband because the outside guards had fled. At midnight, a message came from Monroe, "The enemy are in full march for Washington." Madison left at dawn, promising to be back by three o'clock.

On August 24, the British forced the inexperienced troops guarding the road at Bladensburg to retreat and continued their march toward Washington. The sound of a cannon punctuated the air as Dolley sat down to add another entry to her sister's letter: "Since sunrise I have been turning my spyglass in every direction and watching with unwearied anxiety, hoping to discern the approach of my dear husband and his friends; but alas, I can descry only groups of military wandering in all directions."

Twice during the hot, humid day, the mayor went to the President's House to urge Dolley to depart immediately. She lingered for news of the president. Preparations for dinner continued. About three o'clock, as maid Sukey watched out an upstairs window, Madison's messenger galloped up to the house waving his hat and shouting: "Clear out! Clear out!" Dolley ordered the wagon to be filled with the four large crates containing Madison's papers, a few books, the mansion silver, the red velvet draperies, and a treasured clock. The confusion did not deter her letter writing. She told Lucy about the wagon: "I have had it filled with plate and the most valuable portable articles belonging to the house; whether it will reach its destination, the Bank of Maryland, or fall into the hands of British soldiers, events must determine."

Before she fled, Dolley rescued the portrait of George Washington that hung in the state dining room. She described the dismantling: "Our kind friend, Mr. Carroll, has come to hasten my departure, and he is in a very bad humor with me because I insist on waiting until the large picture of General Washington is secured . . . I have ordered the frame to be broken and the canvas be taken out."

Dolley saved this portrait of George Washington from the British.
(Courtesy of the Library of Congress.)

Her instructions to the two passing men who agreed to take the picture to safety were: "Save that picture! Save that picture, if possible; if not possible, destroy it." The time had come to abandon the President's House. Dolley looked around at the beautiful rooms she loved so much and penned a final word to her sister: "It is done . . . And now, dear sister, I must leave this house or the retreating army will make me a prisoner in it . . . When I shall again write to you, or where I shall be tomorrow, I cannot tell."

Twenty years earlier, Dolley fled Philadelphia, seeking refuge from yellow fever. This time, with the British soldiers close behind, she joined the stream of refugees fleeing Washington.

Two hours later, the British stormed into the city. Inside the Capitol, they piled up woodwork for kindling and sprinkled it with rocket powder. When the fire was lit, flames burst through the roof of the Capitol that reddened the night sky.

By 10:30 P.M., the British, under the command of Admiral Sir George Cockburn, reached the President's House. They ate the dinner Dolley had left for Madison and ransacked the mansion. Filing out into the night, the troops tossed flaming oil-soaked rags through the windows. The fire raced hungrily through the rooms until "the whole building was wrapt in flames and smoke."

The morning after the British set Washington ablaze, a fierce hurricane struck the city. Sheets of torrential rain doused the still smoldering flames. The invaders broke up camp and returned to their ships.

The British burned the city of Washington on August 24, 1814.
(Courtesy of the Library of Congress.)

While the British plundered and burned Washington, Dolley made her way to Virginia. Reportedly, she disguised herself as a farm woman and wandered around in a wagon. Her disguise worked so well that innkeeper after innkeeper refused to provide her refuge. After three days of roaming the countryside in search of each other, James and Dolley reunited and returned to the ruined capital.

Chapter Ten

Peace

In mid-February 1815, bells rang out from the church steeples. Cannons boomed. Bonfires blazed. "Peace and Plenty! Peace, Commerce and Prosperity" spread like wildfire all over the country.

The news had reached the city that ten days earlier, General Andrew Jackson's forces had defeated the British at New Orleans. The victory electrified the nation. Two thousand British soldiers were killed, wounded, or captured—most in the first thirty minutes of the two-hour battle. American losses included seven killed and six wounded. The American people had a new war hero in Andrew Jackson. No one in America knew that a peace treaty had been signed at Ghent by a delegation from the United States and the British government two weeks before the Battle of New Orleans. It probably would not have mattered.

The country was still celebrating the victory at New Orleans when a coach pulled by four foaming horses careened down Pennsylvania Avenue. Inside, a messenger from Ghent clutched a parchment document, and on February 14, 1815, President Madison, surrounded by his cabinet, ratified the Treaty of Ghent.

More nationwide celebrations followed. Washington was jubilant. Dolley threw open the doors of the Octagon House—their temporary residence—to the public. She told the servants to light candles in every window. Crowds gathered in to congratulate the president and celebrate. An observer of Dolley "beheld the radiance of joy which lighted up her countenance and diffused its beams around that all uncertainty was at an end and the government of the country had, in truth . . . 'passed from gloom to glory.' "

Outside, people rejoiced, surging up and down the streets. They passed by the blackened ruins of buildings. That night, triumphal torches lit the sky, which six months before had reflected the flames of the burning city.

Shortly after the war ended, the Madisons' popularity surged. The end of "Mr. Madison's War" turned into "Mr. Madison's peace." Stories of Dolley's efforts to preserve the nation's treasures at the risk of her own life circulated across the country. When war heroes and veterans came to town, she spoke to the troops, boosting morale.

With peace established once again, Dolley rebounded from a period of depression and resumed her entertaining. Dolley's return to the ravaged city in August had been heartbreaking. The loss of personal and public property left her dejected. Visitors reported her "very violent against the English," wishing them "to the bottomless pit." At tea with friends, she sobbed uncontrollably from the stress of the traumatic flight and loss of the President's House.

In December 1814, Dolley shared her sorrow over the burning of the President's House with a friend. "I confess that I was so unfeminine as to be free from fear, and willing to remain in the *Castle*! If I could have had a cannon through every window . . . I remained three days out of town, but I cannot tell you what I felt on re-entering it—such destruction—such confusion."

Dolley and the president received and entertained extensively in the small but elegant Octagon House. "My brain has been harried with noise and bustle," she wrote in March 1815. "Such overflowing rooms I never saw before—I sigh for repose."

The weary Madisons left Washington at the end of March—earlier than usual. Dolley hoped that Payne would join them at Montpelier. His trunks filled with clothes and artwork arrived—but no Payne. He had missed the boat.

Then, one day in late summer, Payne walked though the door at Montpelier after more than two years overseas. He had picked up French manners, French taste, and continued to spend more money than he had. James was hard pressed to pay off Payne's mounting debts, often secretly to keep Dolley from worrying. Eventually Payne's debts would twice land him in debtor's prison, but for now Dolley's charming, wayward son would be returning to Washington with them.

The President's House after the British attack.
(Courtesy of the Library of Congress.)

In October, the Madisons returned to Washington—not to the Octagon House but to the Seven Buildings on Pennsylvania Avenue at Nineteenth Street. This house, with thirty-one windows, hugged the street. Dolley had only to look out the window to see the charred frame of the president's mansion being painted white. One hundred years later, it would officially be named the White House.

Dolley redecorated the Seven Buildings, largely with borrowed furniture or items purchased in local shops. Payne administered the government funds for the refurbishing project. Dolley hoped the responsibility would keep her son from indulging in his expensive habits of gambling and drinking.

Congress focused on the rebuilding of the capital.

James Hoban, Washington's first architect, was called back to restore the capital buildings and the President's House.

One of the more tragic losses of the Capitol fire was the first congressional library. The British burned most of the books, housed at that time on the lower floor of the building. Thomas Jefferson, a great lover and collector of books, grieved over this misfortune. He offered to sell his library, numbering between nine and ten thousand volumes, to Congress to replace the government's loss. Congress set the price at about twenty-four thousand dollars. Jefferson wrote to a friend on May 8, 1815, "Our 10th and last wagon load goes off today . . . unquestionably the choicest collection of books in the U.S. "

With the city well on its way to being rebuilt, Washington society rebounded in the autumn of 1815. Dolley launched her most brilliant season. Her crowded receptions continued to be the highlight of Washington life. To enhance the inadequate lighting in the temporary residence, Dolley placed servants before the drawing room windows, holding aloft blazing pine torches. So brilliant was the illumination that the house would be remembered as "the house of the thousand candles."

The Madisons entertained General Andrew Jackson, the hero of the Battle of New Orleans, on his triumphant visit to Washington. Guests crammed the president's quarters to overflowing to catch a glimpse. It is likely that Dolley's entertainment included a new song that was sweeping the country:

Oh, say can you see, by the dawn's early light,
What so proudly we hailed at the twilight's last
    gleaming?
Whose broad stripes and bright stars, through the
    perilous fight,
O'er the ramparts we watched, were so gallantly
    streaming?
And the rockets' red glare, the bombs bursting in
    air,
Gave proof through the night that our flag was still
    there.
O say, does that star-spangled banner yet wave
O'er the land of the free and the home of the brave?

Shortly after the burning of Washington, Admiral Cockran's fleet had bombarded Baltimore's Fort Henry. Young lawyer Francis Scott Key, acting as Madison's messenger, watched the entire battle from the deck of a British ship where he was detained. At the sight of the battered American flag still waving over the fort the next morning, he wrote "The Star Spangled Banner."

Along with the socializing and rebuilding, Washingtonians engaged in community projects. An orphanage was set up for the city's destitute children, and Dolley became its first director. The ladies of the city spent much of that first winter after the war cutting and sewing children's clothes. Dolley also donated "$20.00 and a cow" to the orphans' cause.

Dolley's love for children was not limited to orphans. Everyday a crowd gathered outside the corner window to watch as Dolley fed and talked to her macaw. The children loved the colorful bird's antics.

Meanwhile Dolley, at the top of her popularity, enjoyed her last season as first lady. For her 1816 New Year's reception, crowds poured in, eager to see Dolley's latest fashion. She chose a yellow satin gown embroidered with butterflies and wore her trademark turban— a feathered creation.

At a reception for the justices of the Supreme Court, the Peace Commission, generals, and the diplomatic corps, Dolley outshone the gold-encrusted uniforms, medals, and ribbons of her guests in her rose-colored gown with a "mile-long" white velvet train lined with lavender satin, and her white turban. Wherever Dolley appeared, she stole the show. At an 1816 Assembly ball, people stood on benches to get a better view. One guest reported that it took ten minutes to "push and shove" his way across the room. Ordinarily, she wore light colors or white—her all time favorite. On this unforgettable evening, she stunned everybody by appearing in a dramatic black velvet dress trimmed in gold and wearing a tiara set with twenty-three sapphires, a gift from James.

Unaccustomed ease characterized the final year of Madison's presidency. When time came for him to leave office, he received praise from many people. One resolution read, "We shall never forget that when our city felt the tempest of war, it was your wisdom and firmness that repaired the breach." Former President John Adams concluded that Madison's administration, "has acquired more glory, and established more Union, than all three predecessors, Washington, Adams and Jefferson, put together."

Outwardly, Dolley showed no regrets at leaving the public stage, where she had played a star role for sixteen years. Her friend from childhood, Eliza Collins Lee (who had now married), told her: "Talents such as yours were never intended to remain inactive . . . As you retire you will carry with you principles and manners not to be put off with the robe of state."

Chapter Eleven

The Last Years

One month after their friend James Monroe became the fifth president of the United States, on March 4, 1817, Dolley and James Madison sailed down the Potomac toward Montpelier on a new steamboat.

The Madisons settled into their remodeled, spacious home. Sixty-six-year-old Madison again took over the full management of his country estate. Because his fields of grain and tobacco were so successful, James and Dolley lived comfortably for the first years of their retirement. Dolley remarked, "I find it most agreeable to stay at home, everything around me is so beautiful."

Dolley Madison provided the same bountiful hospitality for the streams of visitors to Montpelier as she had in Washington. At a Fourth of July picnic, ninety people dined at one table "fixed on the lawn, under a thick arbor." Another time, they had twenty-three overnight guests. Some guests stayed four or five weeks. Distinguished guests included Thomas Jefferson, Daniel

Webster, John Quincy Adams, Andrew Jackson, and Martin Van Buren. The procession of guests added to the enjoyment of country life and kept the Madisons up to date on national politics.

Marquis de Lafayette, who had helped the Americans win the Revolutionary War, made a grand tour of the United States in 1824. He visited the Madisons, and Dolley, meeting him for the first time, found the French general to be enchanting. He and James talked about old times and the current affairs of the United States and France.

Madison told Lafayette that he was editing and re-copying, with the help of Dolley, his detailed notes from the Constitutional Convention. Madison expected the sale of the papers to provide financial security for his wife. Moreover, he wanted to preserve for future Americans a record of the nation's beginning.

All this entertaining was delightful, and expensive. James said that he and Dolley might be "eaten out of house and home." Ten years after retiring from public life, Madison confessed, "Having no resources but in the earth I cultivate, I have been living very much throughout on borrowed means."

The 1820s and 1830s were hard times for most Virginia planters. An agricultural depression caused huge losses; both Jefferson and Monroe went broke. Payne Todd's mounting debts helped to drain the Madisons' resources. James sold his Kentucky lands and mortgaged half of the estate to cover Payne's gambling and drinking debts. Payne attempted to raise silkworms.

When that fell through, he tried mining for marble. Like the silkworms, the mining project was a disaster. After bringing home a few rocks for his parents to admire, Payne drifted off again to pile up more debts. Although her child's absences and failures saddened Dolley, she never stopped loving him: "My poor boy. Forgive his eccentricities—his heart is right."

In the summer of 1828, Margaret Bayard Smith visited Montpelier for the second time. This time, she brought along her little daughter Anna to visit her old friends. "We went over the last twenty years . . . These reminiscences were delightful," Mrs. Smith wrote. On the portico after dinner, sixty-year-old Dolley took Anna by the hand saying, "Come, let us run a race. I do not believe you can outrun me. Madison and I often run races here when the weather does not allow us to walk."

The mistress of Montpelier never lost interest in fashion. Dolley wrote to niece Dolley Cutts, still living in Washington, "Can you send me a paper pattern of the present sleeve, and describe the width of dress and waist; also how turbans are pinned up, and bonnets worn?"

Dolley may have left the bustle of Washington, but she still understood the power of jewels. Young William Cabell Rives and his wife, Judith, visited Montpelier on their way to Washington for his first congressional term. Dolley gave Judith some pieces of her own jewelry, telling her to wear them in Washington society. She explained that her friends would recognize these pieces and know that Judith "moved under Dolley's blessings."

Over the years, as James and Dolley rearranged Madison's historical papers, family members and old friends passed away. The deaths of John Adams and Thomas Jefferson on July 4, 1826, saddened the Madisons and the nation. Jefferson and Madison had enjoyed a close friendship for fifty years. Madison succeeded Jefferson as rector of the University of Virginia. In 1829, Madison's mother, who occupied one wing of Montpelier, died at the age of ninety-eight, and James Monroe died on July 4, 1831. Dolley was devastated by the death of her beloved sister Anna Cutts in 1832.

As the years passed, Madison felt the urgent need to get his notes in shape for publication. He worried that the slavery issue could break up the Union. Although he was often bedridden with arthritis, he continued to work. In the months when he could not write, Dolley sat at his bedside and took notes.

Not only did Madison have health problems, Dolley suffered from eye trouble, and her brother John Payne and three clerks had to assist with the copying. In the summer of 1833, Annie Payne, John's daughter, began her stay with the Madisons, as nurse, private secretary, and daughter, for as long as they both lived.

As Madison grew more frail, Dolley wrote, "My days are devoted to nursing and comforting my sick patient." Eighty-five-year-old James Madison died on June 28, 1836. Again, as when her first husband, John Todd, had died so many years before, Dolley struggled with grief and dire finances.

Finally, in 1837, with the help of William Cabell Rives, Dolley sold three volumes of Madison's recorded debates from the Constitutional Convention to Congress for thirty thousand dollars. Of this amount, she received nine thousand dollars; the remainder went to settle Madison's debts.

Returning to Washington in the fall of 1837, Dolley said, "I seemed suddenly to have awakened after a dream of twenty years, to find myself surrounded by strangers." Accompanied by Annie Payne, she moved into the former Cutts' house—owned by Dolley and debt free—on Lafayette Square. Only now did Dolley discover after many years that Madison had spent forty thousand dollars paying off Payne's debts, and that during some of his long absences Payne had lingered in debtor's prison. Though saddened and horrified by the revelation, Dolley left her incompetent son in charge of running Montpelier.

Dolley reentered Washington society at the age of seventy "like the Queen of this new world." Dolley entertained friends, admirers, and the curious in the house on Lafayette Square. She hosted her traditional open houses on New Year's Day and the Fourth of July. To better afford the entertaining, Dolley lived frugally and skimped on her own meals. Too impoverished to keep up with the latest fashions, she clung to her outdated turbans. The widow always wore black, a sign of mourning and a disguise for the lack of gowns in her once overflowing wardrobe.

The move to Washington eased Dolley's loneliness,

Dolley's niece Annie Payne lived with her during her last years.
(Courtesy of the Greensboro Historical Museum.)

but did nothing to ease her financial stress. Under Payne's mismanagement, Montpelier piled up more debts. Dolley's son plunged deeper into alcoholism. He spent most of his time rolled up in a blanket before the fireplace. When Dolley arrived for the summer in 1839, she hoped to salvage the estate from the wreck Payne had made of it—but it was too late.

Desperate for money, Dolley moved back to Washington and took out a loan on the Lafayette Square house in 1842. She had to sell a large portion of the plantation and rent out the house to pay Payne's gambling and drinking debts. In 1844, she sold the remaining estate. Her dream of passing Montpelier to her son was gone. "Oh, for my counselor!" she often mourned.

Her economic woes and heartbreak did not keep Dolley from participating in important events. The esteemed former first lady was the first woman ever given a permanent seat in the gallery of the House of Representatives. She was a guest of Samuel Morse when the first telegram was sent. She sent the first personal message in Morse code to her cousin in Baltimore. Dolley helped raise money for the Washington monument and participated in the laying of the cornerstone. She acted as a patron for a ball to raise money for needy children.

Dolley was on board the *Princeton* as a presidential guest when an explosion rocked the ship in 1844. She suffered no injuries, but out of several hundred of President Tyler's guests, eight were killed and dozens wounded by shrapnel of red-hot metal. Dolley never talked about her experience.

Dolley remained an active hostess to the end—even in her poverty. Her neighbor Daniel Webster often sent "a market-basket full of provisions" to the Lafayette Square house. Not able to buy gifts for her friends, she gave them pieces of her French china.

Three weeks before Congress made the final decision on Madison's papers, they were almost destroyed. A loud knock on her chamber door awoke Dolley from a sound sleep. A servant yelled, "The house is on fire!" Dolley refused to leave the house until the "trunk of papers" had been rescued from the crackling fire. For the second time, Dolley prevented her husband's papers from being lost.

Finally, on May 20, 1848, Dolley's eightieth birthday, Congress agreed to buy the rest of James Madison's papers for twenty-five thousand dollars. The offer included a provision for Dolley to receive five thousand dollars immediately. The rest would go into a trust fund, so that her son could not spend it. More important to Dolley than her own welfare was that Madison's wish had been fulfilled.

Dolley attended her last White House reception in February 1849. She wore a low-necked white satin gown with a white-fringed turban. President Polk noted, "I passed through the crowded rooms with the venerable Mrs. Madison on my arm."

By summer, Dolley lay critically ill. Payne visited his bedridden mother—not out of the goodness of his heart but out of greed. He pressured Dolley to sign a bogus will, leaving the trust fund entirely to him. A few days later, she realized her mistake and made a new will. This document divided the trust fund equally between faithful Annie and her son.

On July 12, 1849, indomitable eighty-one-year-old Dolley Payne Todd Madison died in her sleep. Annie and her best friend Eliza Collins Lee were at her bedside during the final hours. Major newspapers and telegraph wires carried the news to the world outside of Washington.

The little Quaker girl, who strolled through the Virginia countryside longing for beautiful things, grew up to be a national figure. Her long and full life spanned the terms of twelve presidents. Dolley made a lasting impression on the manners, culture, and political history of a new nation and saved some of its most valuable treasures for future generations.

At Dolley Madison's elaborate funeral service, President Zachary Taylor declared, "She will never be forgotten because she truly was our first lady for half a century."

Timeline

1768—Dolley Payne born on May 20 in North Carolina

1769—Payne family returns to Virginia

1783—Payne family moves to Philadelphia

1790—Dolley Payne marries lawyer John Todd

1792—Gives birth to first child, John Payne Todd

1793—Gives birth to second child, William Temple Todd; husband, John Todd, and son William Temple die

1794—Marries Congressman James Madison

1797—Moves to Montpelier in Virginia

1801—Serves as hostess for President Thomas Jefferson; becomes social leader of the new capital

1805—Spends three months in Philadelphia being treated for a knee infection

1809—Becomes first lady; redecorates the White House

1813—James Madison begins his second term as president

1814—Dolley Madison saves valuable papers and portrait before the British burn the White House

1817—Retires with James Madison to Montpelier

1836—James Madison dies on June 28

1837—Moves back to Washington; sells first three volumes of Madison's papers to Congress

1839—Returns to Montpelier to farm

1841—Returns to Washington
1842—Mortgages her house in Washington; sells part of Mont-
     pelier
1844—Given a permanent seat in Congressional Hall; sells
     the balance of Montpelier
1848—Sells the rest of Madison's papers to Congress
1849—Dies on July 12

Sources

CHAPTER ONE: Quaker Maid

p. 9, "ugly freckles" Noel B. Gerson, *The Velvet Glove* (New York: Thomas Nelson, Inc., 1975), 19.

p. 14, "unanimously agreed that . . ." Katherine Anthony, *Dolly Madison: Her Life and Times* (Garden City, N.Y.: Doubleday and Company, Inc., 1949), 14.

p. 14, "We ought to lament and deplore . . ." Ibid.

CHAPTER TWO: Life in Philadelphia

p. 15, "In my first thirty minutes . . ." Gerson, *Velvet Glove*, 27.

p. 16, "All is well." Anthony, *Life and Times*, 22.

p. 18,"she came upon our cold hearts in Philadelphia . . ." Virginia Moore, *The Madisons* (New York: McGraw-Hill Book Company, 1979), 7.

p. 20, "being of slight figure, possessing . . ." Anthony, *Life and Times*, 31.

p. 20, "You are the most beautiful young lady . . ." Gerson, *Velvet Glove*, 44.

p. 20, "never meant to marry." ed. Lucia Cutts, *Memoirs and Letters of Dolley Madison* (Port Washington, N.Y.: Kennikat Press, 1886), 10.

CHAPTER THREE: Marriage to John Todd

p. 26, "There is no other infant . . ." Gerson, *Velvet Glove*, 52.

p. 29, "uncommonly numerous" Anthony, *Life and Times*, 46.

p. 29, "Parents desert their children . . ." Ibid.

p. 29, "Everyone is leaving the city . . ." Cutts, *Memoirs and Letters*, 12.

p. 30, "I feel the fever in my veins . . ." Anthony, *Life and Times*, 50.

p. 30, "nearly moneyless having only . . ." Ethel Stephens Arnett, *Mrs. James Madison: The Incomparable Dolley.* (Greensboro, N.C.: Piedmont Press, 1972), 52.

p. 31, "my dear Wife Executrix of this my will," Ibid., 53.

p. 31, "I was hurt my dear Jamy that the Idea . . ." Ibid.

CHAPTER FOUR: Return to the City

p. 33, "much impressed with the great . . ." Gerson, *Velvet Glove*, 59.

p. 33, "Gentlemen would station themselves . . . Ibid.

p. 33, "Really Dolley, thou must hide thy face . . ." Cutts, *Memoirs and Letters*, 14.

p. 34, "Thou must come to me. Aaron . . ." Moore, *The Madisons*, 10.

p. 34, "in a mulberry-colored satin, with a silk tulle . . ." Cutts, *Memoirs and Letters*, 15.

p. 34, "black suit of seemly cut, a white shirt . . ." Gerson, *Velvet Glove*, 63.

p. 36, "Dolley, is it true that you are engaged . . ." Cutts, *Memoirs and Letters*, 15-16.

p. 36, "If it is so . . . he will make thee a good husband . . ." Ibid., 16.

p. 38, "He thinks so much of you in the Day . . ." Arnett, *Incomparable Dolley*, 61.

p. 38, "I cannot express . . ." Ibid.

p. 40, "the man . . . I most admire . . . " Moore, *The Madisons*, 16.

p. 40, "Possum in de Gum Tree." Ibid.

p. 41, "Evening. Dolley Madison! Alas!" Arnett, *Incomparable Dolley*, 65.

CHAPTER FIVE: Mrs. James Madison

p. 43, "In about 8 or 10 days we expect to set out . . . " Arnett, *Incomparable Dolley*, 66-67.

p. 44, "a more splendid . . . and officious post." Moore, *The Madisons*, 48.

p. 44, "Present me respectably to Mrs. Madison . . ." Anthony, *Life and Times*, 92.

p. 46, "an odd bird in a Quaker nest." Conover Hunt-Jones, *Dolley and the "great little Madison"* (Washington, D.C.: American Institute of Architects Foundation, 1977), 11.

p. 46, "I went yesterday to see a doll . . . " Gerson, *Velvet Glove*, 80.

p. 47, "will love you as I do, beloved." Ibid., 81.

p. 48, "public business." Marianne Means, *The Woman in the White House* (New York: Random House, 1963), 63.

CHAPTER SIX: "Within a Squirrel's Jump of Heaven"

p. 53, "within a squirrel's jump of Heaven," Maude Wilder Goodwin, *Dolley Madison* (New York: Charles Scribner's Sons, 1896), 61.

p. 54, "two tablecloths large enough . . . " Hunt-Jones, *"great little Madison,"* 20.

p. 55, "Madison chamber." Gerson, *Velvet Glove*, 104.

p. 56, "If you will not save yourself . . ." Moore, *The Madisons*, 148.

p. 57, "we exchanged scarce a word . . ." Gerson, *Velvet Glove*, 105.

p. 58, "Ten for Jefferson . . . " Moore, *The Madisons*, 154.

CHAPTER SEVEN: Washington City Hostess

p. 59, "Yesterday morning rather suddenly . . . " Moore, *The Madisons*, 154.

p. 60, "Let us then, fellow citizens, unite . . ." Ibid., 156.

p. 60, "midnight judges" Ibid., 157.

p. 61, "If they will put me up some bells . . ." Elswyth Thane, *Dolley Madison: Her Life and Times* (New York: The Macmillan Company, 1970).

p. 62, "taking boarders." Anthony, *Her Life and Times*, 112.

p. 63, "It would be hard to overestimate . . . " Ibid., 118.

p. 64, "not merely in an undress, but *actually standing* . . . " Catherine Allgor, *Parlor Politics* (Charlottesville: University Press of Virginia, 2000), 36.

p. 64, "Take Mrs. Merry." Moore, *The Madisons*, 174.

p. 65, "undemocratic diamonds" Allgor, *Parlor Politics*, 45.

p. 66, "One of the greatest griefs of my life has come . . . " Anthony, *Her Life and Times*, 146.

p. 66, "This is among the many proofs . . ." Ibid., 147.

p. 66, "You have no doubt heard of the terrible duel . . . " Goodwin, *Dolley Madison*, 100.

p. 66, "This is a mortal wound . . ." Joseph J. Ellis, *Founding Brothers* (New York: Alfred A. Knoff, 2000), 25.

p. 68, "Mrs. Madison has become one of America's . . . " Gerson, *Velvet Glove*, 158.

p. 68, "sitting still, and amusing myself . . . " Thane, *Dolley Madison: Her Life*, 68.

p. 68, "We are in excellent lodgings . . . "Anthony, *Life and Times*, 168.

p. 69, "I find nothing . . ." Cutts, *Memoirs and Letters*, 56.

p. 69, "Adieu, my beloved, our hearts . . ." Ibid., 57.

p. 69, "My darling husband . . ." Ibid., 59.

p. 70, "they are worshipping the rising sun." Means, *Woman in the White House*, 217.

p. 70, "You are the handsomest woman . . . " Ibid., 200.

p. 71, "indulge me with some information . . . " Ibid.

p. 72, "regardless of dirty politics." Arnett, *Incomparable Dolley*, 98.

CHAPTER EIGHT: Becoming First Lady

p. 73, "extremely beautiful" Margaret Bayard Smith, *The First*

Forty Years of Washington Society, ed. Galliard Hunt, (New York: Charles Scribner's Sons, 1906), 58.

p. 73, "plain cambric dress with . . ." Ibid.

p. 74, "looked a queen. She had on a pale buff . . ." Ibid., 62.

p. 74, "almost pressed to death" Irving Brant, *James Madison, The President 1809-1812* (New York: The Bobbs-Merrill Company, 1956), 14.

p. 74, "moving mass," Ibid.

p. 78, "The curtains! Oh the terrible . . . " Allgor, *Parlor Politics,* 61.

p. 78, "all around the top . . . " Ibid.

p. 79, "distinctly pointed out her station . . ." Paul Zall, *Dolley Madison* (Huntington, N.Y.: Nova History Publications, 2001), 49.

p. 79, "Mrs. Madison's crush" Allgor, *Parlor Politics,* 79.

p. 80, "from dirt and darkness into . . . " Ibid., 76.

p. 80, "is a fine, portly, buxom dame . . ." Ibid.

p. 80, "This is for rough work . . ." Margaret Truman, *First Ladies: An Intimate Group Portrait of White House Wives.* (New York: Fawcett Columbine, 1995), 32.

p. 81, "on the ease with which she . . . " Anthony, *Life and Times,* 197.

p. 82, "unhinged," Allgor, *Parlor Politics,* 80.

p. 82, "houseguests in battalions." Moore, *The Madisons,* 227.

p. 83, "I shouldn't have known . . ." Allgor, *Parlor Politics,* 228.

CHAPTER NINE: The Burning of Washington

p. 84, "I believe there will be . . ." Moore, *The Madisons,* 255.

p. 85, "Mr. Madison's War" Ibid., 275.

p. 85, "I will ask the favor of you to send me . . . " Cutts, *Memoirs and Letters,* 83.

p. 86, "Without Dolley, Madison would . . ." Truman, *First Ladies,* 21.

p. 88, "as I would an infant" Holly Cowan Shulman, "Dolley

(Payne Todd) Madison" *American First Ladies*, ed. Gould, Lewis L., (New York: Garland Publishing, Inc., 1996), 52.

p. 88, "Sometimes I despair . . ." Moore, *The Madisons*, 290.

p. 89, "The fort is being repaired . . . " Thane, *Dolley Madison: Her Life*, 96.

p. 89, "We have met the enemy . . . " Moore, *The Madisons*, 294.

p. 89, "In case of an attack . . . " Anthony, *Life and Times*, 216.

p. 90, "constantly retarded." Ibid.

p. 90, "Dear Sister—My husband left me . . . " Ibid., 224.

p. 91, "The last is alarming, because . . ." Allen C. Clark, *Life and Letters of Dolley Madison* (Washington, D.C.: Press of W.F. Roberts Co., 1914), 164.

p. 91, "Our private property must be sacrificed . . . " Ibid.

p. 91, "The enemy are in full march . . ." Moore, *The Madisons*, 331.

p. 92, "Since sunrise I have been turning . . ." Anthony, *Life and Times*, 224.

p. 92, "Clear out! Clear out!" Ibid., 240.

p. 92, "I have had it filled with plate . . . " Moore, *The Madisons*, 316.

p. 92, "Our kind friend, Mr. Carroll . . ." Anthony, *Life and Times*, 225.

p. 94, "Save that picture . . . " Allgor, *Parlor Politics*, 95.

p. 94, "It is done . . ." Moore, *The Madisons*, 317.

p. 94, "the whole building was wrapt . . . " Zall, *Dolley Madison*, 60.

CHAPTER TEN: Peace

p. 96, "Peace and Plenty! Peace . . . " Mead Minnigerode, *Some American Ladies* (Freeport, N.Y.: Books for Libraries Press, 1969), 126.

p. 97, "beheld the radiance . . . " Goodwin, *Dolley Madison*, 186.

p. 97, "Mr. Madison's War" Anthony, *Life and Times*, 245.

p. 97, "Mr. Madison's peace." Ibid.

p. 98, "very violent against . . ." Zall, *Dolley Madison*, 64.

p. 98, "to the bottomless pit." Ibid.

p. 98, "I confess that . . ." Anthony, *Life and Times*, 230.

p. 98, "My brain has been harried . . ." Gerson, *Velvet Glove*, 226.

p. 100, "Our 10th and last wagon load . . . " Elizabeth Lippincott Dean, *Dolley Madison: The Nation's Hostess* (Boston: Lothrop, Lee & Shepard Co., 1928), 149.

p. 100, "the house of the thousand candles." Moore, *The Madisons*, 360.

p. 101, "O say can you see, by the dawn's . . ." Ibid., 332.

p. 101, "$20.00 and a cow" Dean, *Nation's Hostess*, 157.

p. 102, "mile-long" Ibid., 360.

p. 102, "push and shove" Ibid., 157.

p. 102, "We shall never forget . . ." Irving Brant, *The Fourth President: A Life of James Madison* (New York: The Bobbs-Merrill Company, 1970), 602.

p. 102, "has acquired more glory . . ." Ibid.

p. 103, "Talents such as yours . . ." Paul F. Boller Jr., *Presidential Wives* (New York: Oxford University Press, 1988), 43.

CHAPTER ELEVEN: The Last Years

p. 104, "I find it most agreeable . . . " Zall, *Dolley Madison*, 69.

p. 104, "fixed on the lawn . . ." Thane, *Dolley Madison: Her Life*, 136.

p. 105, "eaten out of house and home." Arnett, *Incomparable Dolley*, 311.

p. 105, "Having no resources . . ." Zall, *Dolley Madison,* 73.

p. 106, "My poor boy . . . " Moore, *The Madisons*, 404.

p. 106, "We went over the last . . ." Smith, *First Forty Years*, 234.

p. 106, "Come, let us run a race . . ." Ibid., 237.

p. 106, "Can you send me a paper pattern . . . " Ibid.

p. 106, "moved under Dolley's blessings." Allgor, *Parlor Politics*, 92.

p. 107, "My days are devoted . . . " Shulman, *American First Ladies*, 64.

p. 108, "I seemed suddenly to have awakened . . . " Zall, *Dolley Madison*, 83.

p. 108, "like the Queen of this . . . " Ibid., 84.

p. 110, "Oh, for my counselor!" Brant, *Fourth President*, 643.

p. 111, "a market-basket full of provisions" Zall, *Dolley Madison*, 97.

p. 111, "The house is on fire!" Arnett, *Incomparable Dolley*, 376.

p. 111, "trunk of papers" Zall, *Dolley Madison*, 95.

p. 111, "I passed through the crowded . . ." Minnigerode, *Some American Ladies*, 132.

p. 112, "She will never be forgotten . . ." Janet Cawley, "Unforgettable First Ladies." *Biography* (February 2001), 72.

Bibliography

Allgor, Catherine. *Parlor Politics.* Charlottesville: University Press of Virginia, 2000.

Anthony, Katherine. *Dolly Madison: Her Life and Times.* Garden City, N.Y.: Doubleday and Company, Inc., 1949.

Arnett, Ethel Stephens. *Mrs. James Madison: The Incomparable Dolley.* Greensboro, North Carolina: Piedmont Press, 1972.

Boller, Paul F. Jr. *Presidential Wives.* New York: Oxford University Press, 1988.

Brant, Irving. *The Fourth President: A Life of James Madison.* New York: The Bobbs-Merrill Company, 1970.

———. *James Madison, The President 1809-1812.* New York: The Bobbs-Merrill Company, 1956.

Cawley, Janet. "Unforgettable First Ladies." *Biography* (February 2001).

Clark, Allen C., ed. *Life and Letters of Dolley Madison.* Washington, D.C.: Press of W.F. Roberts Co., 1914.

Cutts, Lucia, ed. *Memoirs and Letters of Dolley Madison.* Port Washington, NY: Kennikat Press, 1886.

Dean, Elizabeth Lippincott. *Dolley Madison: The Nation's Hostess.* Boston: Lothrope, Lee & Shepard Co., 1928.

Ellis, Joseph J. *Founding Brothers*. New York: Alfred A. Knoff, 2000.

Gerson, Noel B. *The Velvet Glove*. New York: Thomas Nelson, Inc., 1975.

Goodwin, Maude Wilder. *Dolley Madison*. New York: Charles Scribner's Sons, 1896.

Hunt-Jones, Conover. *Dolley and the "great little Madison."* Washington, D.C.: American Institute of Architects Foundation, 1977.

Klaptor, Margaret Brown. *The First Ladies*. Washington, D.C.: White House Historical Association, 1994.

McConnell, Jane, and Burt McConnell. *Our First Ladies*. New York: Thomas Y. Crowell Company, 1969.

Means, Marianne. *The Woman in the White House*. New York: Random House, 1963.

Minnigerode, Mead. *Some American Ladies*. Freeport, N.Y.: Books for Libraries Press, 1969.

Moore, Virginia. *The Madisons*. New York: McGraw-Hill Book Company, 1979.

Shulman, Holly Cowan. "Dolley (Payne Todd) Madison" in *American First Ladies*. Edited by Lewis L. Gould. New York: Garland Publishing, 1996.

Smith, Margaret Bayard. *The First Forty Years of Washington Society*. Edited by Gaillard Hunt. New York: Charles Scribner's Sons, 1906.

Thane, Elswyth. *Dolley Madison: Her Life and Times*. New York: The Macmillan Company, 1970.

Truman, Margaret. *First Ladies: An Intimate Group Portrait of White House Wives*. New York: Fawcett Columbine, 1995.

Watson, Robert P. *The Presidents' Wives: Reassessing the Office of First Lady*. London: Lynne Rienner Publishers, Inc., 2000.

Zall, Paul. *Dolley Madison*. Huntington, N.Y.: Nova History Publications, 2001.

Websites

The Greensboro Historical Museum
http://www.greensborohistory.org/

National First Ladies Library
http://www.firstladies.org

University of Virginia: The Dolley Madison Project
http://www.vcdh.virginia.edu/madison/index.html

The White House: Biography of Dolley Madison
http://www.whitehouse.gov/history/firstladies/dm4.html

Index